# Jury Manual

## A Guide for Prospective Jurors

by
**William R. Pabst, B.A., J.D.**

*Illustrations by Gary Yokie*

First Edition
March 1985

This project was supported by the Centre for the Independence of Judges and Lawyers of the United States, Inc. The views and opinions expressed herein are the author's and do not necessarily reflect the views, opinions or the official position of the Centre.

Published by Metro Publishing, Houston, Texas
Manufactured in the United States of America
Library of Congress Catalog Card No. 84-72310
ISBN 0-933745-00-1

# Foreword

The awesome power of the jury is the single most ignored concept in the legal procedures of our courts. Throughout the trial process, the judge will refuse to inform you of your rights and powers as a juror. Further, the judge will prohibit the attorneys from explaining your rights to you. Your ignorance of this aspect of the judicial process could transform you into an instrument of injustice and intolerance resulting in the conviction of an innocent person. As you read this book, you will discover the extent of your rights and powers as a juror in the courts of the United States of America. This knowledge will enhance your ability to participate in one of the fundamental institutions of a free society — trial by jury.

# Contents

# History
# of the Jury

There is no record of trial by jury prior to the times of the Anglo-Saxons. However, indications do suggest the beginnings of the basic concept. For example, about 725 A.D. a Welsh king, Morgan of Gla-Morgan, utilized a system named "the Apostolic Law." Based on the Biblical account of Christ and the twelve Apostles, this system was applied to the decision-making practices of that community. The king and twelve wise men would decide how best to resolve a particular dispute.[1]

During this period, certain types of injuries were remedied by the payment of fixed amounts based on a financial formula. The system evolved into a regularly published list of financial penalties replacing the popular system of personal vengeance. The system of personal vengeance operated as one might deduce: when a killing took place, the family members of the victim avenged the murder themselves. This resulted in ever-increasing violence.

A community standard eventually developed which allowed financial compensation for the injury. If the family of the victim refused this option, the guilty person was punished severely. If the murderer, for example, refused to pay compensation, he would suffer the consequences of the injured family's vengeance.[2]

1

Another method for assuring tranquility in the community required each family to pay a specified amount to guarantee that members of the family would keep the peace. The community would be protected from violence through this "insurance" payment.[3]

A different system was employed on other matters which might be considered commercial disputes. Under this system, the accused would obtain a required number of friends, known as compurgators, to swear that he was innocent. This differed from the English system in that the English compugators swore under oath that the accused had not perjured himself when he denied the charges.[4]

Although the number of compurgators varied, the usual number was twelve persons. These persons were not jurors; they were, more accurately, character witnesses. Naturally, the use of friends as compurgators resulted in few trials because most people did not want to act against a friend. In most instances a body of people was chosen from either relatives or people from the same trade as the accused. These people were supposed to be more objective in their decision of the accused person's innocence or guilt.

If the accused could not find enough compurgators to support his position, he was subjected to trial by ordeal. Three types of ordeal were used:    a) The accused had to carry a certain weight of red-hot iron for a certain distance;    b) The accused had to submerge his hand in a container of boiling water in order to remove an object;    c) The accused had to eat a piece of bread while saying a prayer that he may choke if guilty.

Although some modern scholars do not accept the concept that the jury system developed from the practice of using compurgators,[6] the forerunner of the jury as we know it today can be found during the time of Henry II. Again, twelve men were usually chosen, but the number could vary. These juries were still composed primarily of witnesses. The accused, however, retained the option of trial by combat.[7]

During the first year of the reign of King John, taxes levied on the knights were increased. In 1203, a seventh of the barons' movable property was taxed. In 1204, another amount was taken from the knights, and in 1207, a thirteenth of all personal property was taxed. In addition to the pressure of taxation, the baronage was constantly harassed by demands for military service in fruitless "no-win" foreign wars. The northern barons openly refused to serve in military expeditions abroad in 1213, and by doing so refused to follow the king.[8]

The decisive confrontation came at Runnymeade, England in 1215, when King John was forced at the point of a sword to agree to the Magna Carta. Only the wealthy knights and landowners participated in this act. Neither women nor the poor took part in the writing of this first

A proven way to make the government uphold the rights of the people.

3

document outlining the basic rights of man. Women were little more than property and the poor had to labor under inhuman conditions just to have enough to eat.[9]

Four distinct aspects of the Magna Carta are noteworthy. First, Magna Carta stood for the concept that the people could impose their individual will and sovereign power upon the government. This made government the servant rather than the master. Second, Magna Carta stood for the principle that the will of the people regarding their fundamental rights was to be itemized in a written document. Third, Magna Carta stood for the idea that the written document is superior to the legislative and executive power; it is merely a recording of fundamental rights that existed prior to the charter. Fourth, the Magna Carta symbolized the notion that even though it was impossible to enumerate all rights, those not specifically stated were still retained.[10]

In 1819, the U.S. Supreme Court ruled:
> "...as to the words of Magna Carta, incorporated into the Constitution of Maryland, after volumes spoken and written with a view to their exposition, the good sense of mankind has at length settled down to this: that they were intended to secure the individual from the **arbitrary exercise of the powers of government**, unrestrained by the established principles of private rights and distributive justice."[11]

The U.S. Supreme Court has also stated:
> "...dating back to Magna Carta, however, it has been an abiding principle governing the lives of civilized men that under Chapter 39 of the Charter, 'no freeman shall be taken, imprisoned, disseised, outlawed, or in any way destroyed, nor will we proceed against him or prosecute him, **except by the lawful judgment of his peers**, and by the law of the land.'"[12]

The use of jurors who were not witnesses began in 1267, even though a system of basic rights was still unknown to these people. Participation on the jury was based on wealth and property. Neither unlanded individuals nor women were allowed to be jurors.

Throughout this period the government controlled the jury. In some instances if the jury did not arrive at the decision desired by the judge, he punished the jurors severely. Wives and children of jurors were evicted from their homes, which were then destroyed along with the rest of their property.[13]

Obviously, trial by jury in England then was merely a procedural farce used to resolve disputes of the elite and to legitimize oppression of the people by the "official" act of a court and jury totally controlled by the government.

"Must not have been a witch; witches float!"

One of the reasons the American colonies declared independence was the corrupt, tyrannical government of England that had been "depriving us in many cases of the benefits of trial by jury."[14]  Although English common law is praised by so many, our forefathers came to these shores fleeing it and wishing to change it.

In the case of Van Ness v. Pacard (1829) the judge stated:

> "The common law of England is not to be taken in all respects to be that of America. Our ancestors brought with them general principles, and claimed it as their birth-right; but they brought with them and adopted only that portion which was applicable to their condition."[15]

Trial by jury was not accepted by all of the colonies. The laws of England were neither "in the whole nor in any part of them valid or pleadable in the colonial courts until received by the General Assembly."[16] Examples of these modifications in jury systems are evident in the history of the various colonies.

In Connecticut, there was no radical departure from the English system of trial by jury, but divine law prevailed. In New Hampshire and Vermont, the only laws accepted were those of the General Assembly that had been approved by the president and the council. All questions of law and fact were decided by juries.[17]

In Rhode Island, the jury trial practices of England were modified.[18] In New York, jury trials were quite informal. By law in 1729, lawyers were forbidden to be elected representatives to the general assembly; their presence was considered distasteful.[19] In Pennsylvania and Maryland, the colonists were so opposed to the English system of trial by jury that it was greatly modified.[20] In Virginia and the Carolinas, the English statutes regarding rights and liberties as well as the common law were acknowledged except when they conflicted with customs of the colonists.[21]

6

The right to a fair trial by jury, free from government control, was of such great importance that it was mentioned in three places within the U.S. Constitution.

Article III, Clause 3 states:
> The trial of all crimes, . . . , shall be by Jury.

Amendment VI states:
> In all criminal prosecutions, the accused shall enjoy the right to a speedy and public trial, by an impartial jury . . .

Amendment VII further states:
> In all suits at common law, where the value in controversy shall exceed twenty dollars, the right of trial by jury shall be preserved, and no fact tried by a jury, shall be otherwise re-examined in any Court of the United States, than according to the rules of the common law.[22]

As we can see, the jury system developed as an efficient and equitable social method of settling grievances and disputes. Later it evolved into a check on the abuse of governmental power. The authors of our legal structure who created the Constitution and Bill of Rights regarded the jury system as fundamental for the preservation of individual liberty. The emphasis placed on the jury system throughout the history of our country indicates its pivotal position in the American legal structure.

# Understanding Right and Wrong

To be a good juror, you must have a basic concept of right and wrong, as well as an appreciation of what is ethical.

Three excellent documents which assist us in conceptualizing good and rejecting evil are the Bible, the Bill of Rights as contained in the first ten amendments to the Constitution of the United States, and the United Nations' Declaration of Human Rights. You should understand that law can only be judged by applying to it the standards of basic rights and not by blind, unquestioning obedience.

As our society develops, it is not so much the appearance of murder and torture by our government employees that we have to fear. More realistically, we must be aware of the use of the *law* as an instrument of oppression by the governing elite. This manifests itself slowly, over long periods of time. Specific areas of unjust laws are: government regulation of small businesses; drafting young men as cannon fodder to die in a long series of "no-win" wars; taxation that destroys the incentive of the citizen to progress; government interference with religion; laws that prevent you from criticizing the government; and laws interfering with the ownership of firearms — the private

9

ownership of which is our only protection against bureaucrats gone berserk.

The first guideline to follow in our relationships with our fellow human beings is found in the Holy Bible.

St. Matthew, Chapter 7, verses 1 and 2 state:
> *Judge not, that ye be not judged. For with what judgment ye judge, ye shall be judged: and with what measure ye mete, it shall be measured to you again.*[23]

So the danger of sitting in judgment on another is that you are applying the same standards of judgment that will be applied to you. If your basis of judgment is unfair when applied to another, that same unfair standard eventually will be applied to you.

More instructions are found in verse 5:
> *Thou hypocrite, first cast out the beam out of thine own eye; and then shalt thou see clearly to cast out the mote out of thy brother's eye.*[24]

Exodus, Chapter 20, contains the Ten Commandments:
> *And God spake all these words, saying, I am the Lord thy God, which have brought thee out of the land of Egypt, out of the house of bondage. Thou shalt have no other gods before me. Thou shalt not make unto thee any graven image, or any likeness of any thing that is in heaven above, or that is in the earth beneath, or that is in the water under the earth. Thou shalt not bow down thyself to them, nor serve them for I the Lord thy God am a jealous God, visiting the iniquity of the fathers upon the children unto the third and fourth generation of them that hate me; and shewing mercy unto*

"Either find the accused guilty or I will have you all evicted from your homes and your crops burnt. Now do as I tell you — *or else!*"

*thousands of them that love me, and keep my commandments. Thou shalt not take the name of the Lord thy God in vain; for the Lord will not hold him guiltless that taketh his name in vain. Remember the sabbath day, to keep it holy. Six days shalt thou labour and do all thy work. But the seventh day is the sabbath of the Lord thy God. In it thou shalt not do any work, thou, nor thy son, nor thy daughter, thy manservant, nor thy maidservant, nor thy cattle, nor thy stranger that is within thy gates. For in six days the Lord made heaven and earth, the sea and all that in them is, and rested the seventh day. Wherefore the*

11

*Lord blessed the sabbath day, and hallowed it. Honour thy father and thy mother, that thy days may be long upon the land which the Lord thy God giveth thee. Thou shalt not kill. Thou shalt not commit adultery. Thou shalt not steal. Thou shalt not bear false witness against thy neighbour. Thou shalt not covet thy neighbour's house, thou shalt not covet thy neighbour's wife, nor his manservant, nor his maidservant, nor his ox, nor his ass, nor any thing that is thy neighbour's.*[25]

The rule about bearing false witness against your neighbor would apply to the juror in his decision-making process.

Exodus, Chapter 23, provides more rules regarding truth:

*Thou shalt not raise a false report. Put not thine hand with the wicked to be an unrighteous witness. Thou shalt not follow a multitude to do evil; neither shalt thou speak in a cause to decline after many to wrest judgment. Neither shalt thou countenance a poor man in his cause.*[26]

*Thou shalt not wrest the judgment of thy poor in his cause. Keep thee far from a false matter; and the innocent and righteous slay thou not. For I will not justify the wicked.*[27]

*And thou shalt take no gift. For the gift blindeth the wise, and perverteth the words of the righteous. Also thou shalt not oppress a stranger. For ye know the heart of a stranger, seeing ye were strangers in the land of Egypt.*[28]

According to the Bible, then, some very strict rules exist that govern the acts of any juror.

The second document defines the basic rights of man in relation to his government. This document, known as the Bill of Rights, is comprised of the first ten amendments to the Constitution of the United States and has been incorporated into governing documents of democracies around the world. Just as the Bible instructs us on relationships between men, the Bill of Rights, advancing a step beyond the Magna Carta, instructs us on the relationship between men and government. Note how it limits government in a universal manner:

# Bill of Rights

1.   Congress shall make no law respecting an establishment of religion, or prohibiting the free exercise thereof; or abridging the freedom of speech, or of the press; or the right of the people peaceably to assemble, and to petition the Government for a redress of grievances.

2.   A well regulated Militia, being necessary to the security of a free State, the right of the people to keep and bear Arms, shall not be infringed.

3.   No soldier shall, in time of peace be quartered in any house, without the consent of the Owner, nor in time of war, but in a manner to be prescribed by law.

4.   The right of the people to be secure in their persons, houses, papers, and effects, against unreasonable searches and seizures, shall not be violated, and no Warrants shall issue, but upon probable cause, supported by Oath or affirmation, and particularly describing the place to be searched, and the persons or things to be seized.

"You should find this draft dodger guilty.
How can *we* fight a war if *we* can't get people to fight it
for us?"

5. No person shall be held to answer for a
capital, or otherwise infamous crime, unless
on a presentment or indictment of a Grand
Jury, except in cases arising in the land or naval
forces, or in the Militia, when in actual service
in time of War or public danger; nor shall any
person be subject for the same offence to be
twice put in jeopardy of life or limb; nor shall
be compelled in any criminal case to be a witness against himself, nor be deprived of life,
liberty, or property, without due process of
law; nor shall private property be taken for
public use, without just compensation.

6.   In all criminal prosecutions, the accused shall enjoy the right to a speedy and public trial, by an impartial jury of the State and district wherein the crime shall have been committed, which district shall have been previously ascertained by law, and to be informed of the nature and cause of the accusation; to be confronted with the witnesses against him; to have compulsory process for obtaining witnesses in his favor, and to have the Assistance of Counsel for his defence.

7.   In suits at common law, where the value in controversy shall exceed twenty dollars, the right of trial by jury shall be preserved, and no fact tried by a jury, shall be otherwise re-examined in any Court of the United States, than according to the rules of the common law.

8.   Excessive bail shall not be required, nor excessive fines imposed, nor cruel and unusual punishments inflicted.

9.   The enumeration in the Constitution, of certain rights, shall not be construed to deny or disparage others retained by the people.

10.   The powers not delegated to the United States by the Constitution, nor prohibited by it to the States, are reserved to the States respectively, or to the people.[29]

The third related document that you need to be aware of is the Universal Declaration of Human Rights.[30] This document, signed by President Jimmy Carter, is the result of years of work by the member states to the United Nations and contains a listing of the rights of man.

# Universal Declaration of Human Rights

## Preamble

WHEREAS recognition of the inherent dignity and of the equal and inalienable rights of all members of the human family is the foundation of freedom, justice and peace in the world,

WHEREAS disregard and contempt for human rights have resulted in barbarous acts which have outraged the conscience of mankind, and the advent of a world in which human beings shall enjoy freedom of speech and belief and freedom from fear and want has been proclaimed as the highest aspiration of the common people,

WHEREAS it is essential to promote the development of friendly relations between nations,

WHEREAS the peoples of the United Nations have in the Charter reaffirmed their faith in fundamental human rights, in the dignity and worth of the human person and in the equal rights of men and women and have determined to promote social progress and better standards of life in larger freedom,

16

WHEREAS Member States have pledged themselves to achieve, in co-operation with the
United Nations, the promotion of universal respect for an observance of human rights and
fundamental freedoms,

WHEREAS a common understanding of these
rights and freedoms is of the greatest importance for the full realization of this pledge,

Now, therefore, THE GENERAL ASSEMBLY
proclaims this Universal Declaration of Human
Rights as a common standard of achievement
for all peoples and all nations, to the end that
every individual and every organ of society,
keeping this Declaration constantly in mind,
shall strive by teaching and education to promote respect for these rights and freedoms and
by progressive measures, national and international, to secure their universal and effective
recognition and observance, both among the
peoples of Member States themselves and
among the peoples of territories under their
jurisdiction.

## Article 1
All human beings are born free and equal in
dignity and rights. They are endowed with
reason and conscience and should act toward
one another in a spirit of brotherhood.

## Article 2
Everyone is entitled to all the rights and freedoms set forth in this Declaration, without
distinction of any kind, such as race, color, sex,
language, religion, political or other opinion,
national or social origin, property, birth or

other status. Furthermore, no distinction shall be made on the basis of the political, jurisdictional or international status of the country or territory to which a person belongs, whether it be independent, trust, non-self-governing or under any other limitation of sovereignty.

## Article 3
Everyone has the right to life, liberty and security of person.

## Article 4
No one shall be held in slavery or servitude. Slavery and the slave trade shall be prohibited in all their forms.

## Article 5
No one shall be subjected to torture or to cruel, inhuman or degrading treatment or punishment.

## Article 6
Everyone has the right to recognition everywhere as a person before the law.

## Article 7
All are equal before the law and are entitled without any discrimination to equal protection of the law. All are entitled to equal protection against any discrimination in violation of this Declaration and against any incitement to such discrimination.

## Article 8
Everyone has the right to an effective remedy by the competent national tribunals for acts violating the fundamental rights granted him by the constitution or by law.

## Article 9
No one shall be subjected to arbitrary arrest, detention or exile.

## Article 10
Everyone is entitled in full equality to a fair and public hearing by an independent and impartial tribunal, in the determination of his rights and obligations and of any criminal charge against him.

## Article 11
1. Everyone charged with a penal offence has the right to be presumed innocent until proved guilty according to law in a public trial at which he has and all the guarantees necessary for his defense.
2. No one shall be held guilty of any penal offence on account of any act or omission which did not constitute a penal offence, under national or international law, at the time when it was committed.

## Article 12
No one shall be subjected to arbitrary interference with his privacy, family, home or correspondence, nor to attacks upon his honour and reputation. Everyone has the right to the protection of the law against such interference or attacks.

## Article 13
1. Everyone has the right to freedom of movement and residence within the borders of each state.
2. Everyone has the right to leave any country, including his own, and to return to his country.

## Article 14

1.  Everyone has the right to seek and to enjoy in other countries asylum from persecution.
2.  This right may not be invoked in the case of prosecutions genuinely arising from non-political crimes or from acts contrary to the purposes and principles of the United Nations.

## Article 15

1.  Everyone has the right to a nationality.
2.  No one shall be arbitrarily deprived of his nationality nor denied the right to change his nationality.

## Article 16

1.  Men and women of full age, without any limitation due to race, nationality or religion, have the right to marry and to found a family. They are entitled to equal rights as to marriage, during marriage and at its dissolution.
2.  Marriage shall be entered into only with the free and full consent of the intending spouses.
3.  The family is the natural and fundamental group unit of society and is entitled to protection by society and the State.

## Article 17

1.  Everyone has the right to own property alone as well as in association with others.
2.  No one shall be arbitrarily deprived of his property.

## Article 18

Everyone has the right to freedom of thought, conscience and religion; this right includes freedom to change his religion or belief, and freedom, either alone or in community with others and in public or private, to manifest his religion or belief in teaching, practice, worship and observance.

## Article 19

Everyone has the right to freedom of opinion and expression; this right includes freedom to hold opinions without interference and to seek, receive and impart information and ideas through any media and regardless of frontiers.

## Article 20

1.  Everyone has the right to freedom of peaceful assembly and association.
2.  No one may be compelled to belong to an association.

## Article 21

1.  Everyone has the right to take part in the government of his country, directly or through freely chosen representatives.

2.  Everyone has the right of equal access to public service in his country.

3.  The will of the people shall be the basis of the authority of government; this will shall be expressed in periodic and genuine elections which shall be by universal and equal suffrage and shall be held by secret vote or by equivalent free voting procedures.

## Article 22

Everyone, as a member of society, has the right to social security and is entitled to realization, through national effort and international cooperation and in accordance with the organization and resources of each state, of the economic, social and cultural rights indispensable for his dignity and the free development of his personality.

## Article 23

1.   Everyone has the right to work, to free choice of employment, to just and favorable conditions of work and to protection against unemployment.

2.   Everyone, without any discrimination, has the right to equal pay for equal work.

3.   Everyone who works has the right to just and favorable remuneration ensuring for himself and his family an existence worthy of human dignity, and supplemented, if necessary, by other means of social protection.

4.   Everyone has the right to form and to join trade unions for the protection of his interests.

## Article 24

Everyone has the right to rest and leisure, including reasonable limitation of working hours and periodic holidays with pay.

## Article 25

1.   Everyone has the right to a standard of living adequate for the health and well-being of himself and of his family, including food, clothing, housing and medical care and necessary social services, and the right to security in the event of unemployment, sickness, disability, widowhood, old age or other lack of livelihood in circumstances beyond his control.

2.   Motherhood and childhood are entitled to special care and assistance. All children, whether born in or out of wedlock, shall enjoy the same social protection.

## Article 26

1. Everyone has the right to education. Education shall be free, at least in the elementary and fundamental stages. Elementary education shall be compulsory. Technical and professional education shall be made generally available and higher education shall be equally accessible to all on the basis of merit.

2. Education shall be directed to the full development of the human personality and to the strengthening of respect for human rights and fundamental freedoms. It shall promote understanding, tolerance and friendship among all nations, racial or religious groups, and shall further the activities of the United Nations for maintenance of peace.

3. Parents have a prior right to choose the kind of education that shall be given to their children.

## Article 27

1. Everyone has the right freely to participate in the cultural life of the community, to enjoy the arts and to share in scientific advancement and its benefits.

2. Everyone has the right to the protection of the moral and material interests resulting from any scientific, literary or artistic production of which he is the author.

## Article 28

Everyone is entitled to a social and international order in which the rights and freedoms set forth in this Declaration can be fully realized.

## Article 29

1. Everyone has duties to the community in

which alone the free and full development of his personality is possible.

2. In the exercise of his rights and freedoms, everyone shall be subject only to such limitations as are determined by law solely for the purpose of securing due recognition and respect for the rights and freedoms of others and of meeting the just requirements of morality, public order and the general welfare in a democratic society.

3. These rights and freedoms may in no case be exercised contrary to the purposes and principles of the United Nations.

## Article 30

Nothing in this Declaration may be interpreted as implying for any State, group or person any right to engage in any activity or to perform any act aimed at the destruction of any of the rights and freedoms set forth herein.

The information in this chapter is provided to assist you, as a juror, in arriving at a fair and just consideration of the information that will be presented to you during a trial. Your ability to appraise a particular situation must come from your basic knowledge of what is right or wrong.

# Rights and Powers
# of the Jury

Jury nullification refers to the right of a jury, sitting as representatives of the community conscience, to disregard the strict requirements of a law where the jury finds that those requirements cannot be applied justly and fairly to an accused person. When the jury refuses to convict under these circumstances, it is stating that the acts of the accused were justified, regardless of the law.

This concept is also called the *jury veto* because the jury, by refusing to convict a person, is *vetoing* a law that cannot be fairly applied to the case. In other words, the person accused may be guilty of violating the law, but the jury may find him not guilty because the jury feels the law is unfair or unjust.

**The jury has the undisputed power to acquit, even if its verdict is contrary to the evidence.** This is a power that must exist as long as we adhere to the general verdict in criminal cases; the courts cannot search the minds of the jurors to find the basis upon which they judge. If the jury feels that the law under which the defendant is accused is unjust, or that more important circumstances justified the actions of the accused, or if any other reason appeals to their logic or passion, the jury has the power to acquit, and the courts must abide by that decision.[31]

This power exists for the simple reason that governments traditionally use courts to oppress and terrorize the people. It is usually a simple matter for a judge or a government attorney to bully ordinary citizens into making a decision that the juror feels deep within his soul is wrong. The historical case of John Peter Zenger serves as the standard for this fear.

Zenger was accused of writing statements against the government, a violation of the law at that time. He was, in fact, guilty of the charges brought against him. But Andrew Hamilton urged the jury, in spite of the judge's instructions, to "see with their own eyes, to hear with their own ears, and to make use of their consciences and understanding in judging of the lives, liberties, or estates" of their fellow countrymen.[32]

"I can't help it if you didn't understand the case.
Reach a decision or I'll keep you here forever!"

The jury would not find Zenger guilty. The judge threatened the jurors; he attempted to force them to make a decision against their consciences and own good judgment. They, nevertheless, stood their ground, refused to be bullied by the judge, and found Zenger "Not Guilty."

In another famous case, William Penn and William Mead were accused by the government of preaching the word of God to a group of people who had gathered on a street to listen. The law stated that it was illegal for people to gather in the street to listen to a preacher.[33]

At the trial that ensued, the jury refused to find the two preachers guilty. The judge was infuriated because he was accustomed to having jurors act as puppets to produce whatever verdict he desired. The judge, seeing that the jurors were not cowards, began to abuse them. He deprived them of food, drink, fire and tobacco and told them that they would stay in jail until they starved unless they issued the guilty verdict he wanted.[34]

When the judge finally realized that he was not going to be able to force the jury to make a decision against their conscience, he accepted their verdict of "Not Guilty" but held them in jail anyway, stating that they were jailed for contempt of court. Those who could pay their fines were released.[35]

These and other cases demonstrate the courage with which jurors have responded to the tyranny of the judiciary throughout history.

For about fifty years after the American Revolution, juries determined the law and the facts in cases. But the judges wanted to preserve the powers over the citizenry that they had enjoyed before the revolution. Since these judges had no legislative authority, they began to insist that *they* would determine what the law was during the trial; the jury would determine only the facts of the case.[36]

In the Dean of St. Asaph's Case (1783) the court stated:

> "The jury, by means of a general verdict, is entrusted with a power of blending law and fact, and of following the prejudices of their affections or passions. It is the duty of the judge, in all cases of general justice, to tell the jury how to do right, though they have it in their power to do wrong, which is entirely between God and their own consciences."[37]

John Jay was the first chief justice of the U.S. Supreme Court and assisted in obtaining the ratification of the Constitution. During the Revolutionary War, he wrote in the Federalist Papers. President of the Continental Congress from 1778 to 1779, he helped negotiate the Treaty of Peace with England after the Revolutionary War. John Jay can provide guidance on the rights of a juror because he participated not only in the revolutionary period but in the structuring of our government:

> "It may not be amiss, here, Gentlemen, to remind you of the good old rule, that on questions of fact, it is the province of the jury, on questions of law, it is the province of the court to decide. But it must be observed that by the same law, which recognizes this reasonable distribution of jurisdiction, you have nevertheless a right to take upon yourselves to judge of both, and to determine the law as well as the fact in controversy. On this, and on every other occasion, however, we have no doubt, you will pay that respect, which is due to the opinion of the court; for, as on the one hand, it is presumed, that juries are the best judges of facts; it is, on the other hand, presumable, that the courts are the best judges of law. But still both objects are lawfully, within your power of decision."[38]

**The jury has the power to reach a verdict in spite of both law and facts.** This power of the jury is fundamental

28

in a free society because it gives people the final determination of whether a law is fair.[39] The jury has the undisputed power to acquit, even if its verdict is contrary to law as given by the judge and contrary to evidence.[40]

The judge can enlighten the understanding of the jury and thereby influence its judgment; but he cannot use undue influence. He can advise; he can persuade; but he cannot command or coerce.[41]

The rights of jurors can be better understood by examining some U.S. laws. Prior to the Civil War, anti-slavery sentiment was very high in the northern United States. A majority of our representatives in the Congress were pro-slavery and promoted slavery as an institution. This bias was apparent in the Fugitive Slave Act of 1850,[42] which provided that slave owners or their representatives could go into other states where slaves had fled from bondage and capture them for return to their "owners." No court procedure was necessary, and the slave enjoyed no protection by the government whatsoever. The "owner" would merely go to a federal commissioner appointed to process such matters and present title papers or an affidavit of ownership; the slave could not defend himself. So by the use of federal law, the slave would be returned to his "owner." There was, however, a fine of $1,000 and a jail sentence of six months for anyone who tried to help the slave obtain freedom. In addition, the federal commissioner in charge of the procedure received $10 for each slave he returned to the "owner." When a search for a slave was under way, anyone who happened to be standing around could be forced by government officials to assist in the capture of the slave, regardless of how he or she felt about the government-protected institution of slavery.
Many people of conscience were irritated that their government was promoting and preserving such an evil, so they began to commit acts against the government as a

manifestation of their disagreement with the official pro-slavery policy. Joshua Giddings, a congressman, explained to the House of Representatives that the people should feel there was a higher law than the Fugitive Slave Act and that was the law of "right, of justice, of freedom" which is found within the heart of all respectable people and which makes them look with disrespect upon such legislation.

A Presbyterian minister, Lyman Beecher, preached about the duty of the people regarding the Fugitive Slave Act in his sermon *The Duty of Disobedience to Wicked Laws*[43]. Even today, his words apply directly to what a juror should do if he is being pressured into finding someone guilty of violating a law that the juror feels is unjust or evil:

> "No human laws are of any validity if contrary to the law of nature."

Because there were penalties for helping escaped slaves, Beecher analyzed the problem of what to do if a slave woman and her children arrived at your house on a dark, cold night. He asked:

> "What does the law require of you? What must you do to obey this law? You must shut your door in her face, or you must take her captive and shut her up until the hounds and officers can come up. This is obedience; and if you do not do this you are a law-breaker. If you give her a crust of bread you break the law. If you give her a shawl, a cloak; if you let her warm herself by your fire an hour, you break the law. I know it is wrong, abstractly considered, you say; but the law says so, and I must do it till the law is altered. True, it seems to me wrong, but what right have I to set up my judgment against the Law? True, it seems to me that this law conflicts with the Golden Rule, on which

hang all the Law and the prophets, and nullifies all principles of honor and humanity, but what right have I to follow my own private impressions of right against the laws of the land? What right have I to say I will obey the laws of the land just so far as they coincide with my ideas of right, but when they do not, I will break them? If everybody should do so, would it not put an end to all law, and disorganize society? No, No; I must try to get this law repealed, but in the meanwhile I must keep it, even if it command me to violate every principle of the Decalogue *(The Ten Commandments)."*

Reverend Beecher provided the answer once and for all to this question, which must arise in the minds of all good-thinking citizens whenever their government attempts to make them into accomplices of evil:

"Here is the stereotyped argument for all such cases made and provided which has been used by civil and religious despotism in all ages. First, pass a law that compels men to violate conscience, and then drive them to keep it by conscience. The worst of it is that these profligate preachers of integrity cheat their hearers by a fallacy, a falsehood so slyly slipped in, as to escape detection. They misrepresent the whole position of conscientious men. They represent us as if we claimed the right to violate any law that might happen not to suit our convenience, or our notions of propriety. They say that our claim of the right to violate one law, which we consider wrong, is a warrant for the violation of all laws, right or wrong. Now, this is a false conclusion. It represents us confounding the distinction between laws which are simply injurious or inexpedient, and those which are positively sinful."

Reverend Beecher continued:

> "I may disapprove a law, I may think it unwise, injudicious, . . . and yet it may not require me to do anything positively wrong. I may submit to such a law, innocently, because I wrong nobody. But here is a law which commands me to sin positively and without apology. It commands me, when fully obeyed, to deny Christ, to renounce and abjure Christ's law, to trample under foot Christ's Spirit, and to remand Christ's flesh and blood into cruel bondage."

He then stated:

> "A law which does me some injury is one thing. A law which makes me do wrong is another. The first I may submit to while seeking its repeal. To the latter I must not give place by subjection, no, not for an hour. I must resist unto blood, striving against sin, i.e., to the patient shedding of my own blood. Hence, to disobey such a law does not disorganize society. It does not unsettle law."

And concluded:

> "...the men that refuse obedience to such laws are the sure, the only defenders of law. If they will shed their own blood rather than sin by keeping a wicked law, they will by the same principle shed their blood rather than break a law which is righteous. In short, such men are the only true law-abiding men."

Theodore Parker, another minister, spoke in similar fashion about the plight of a juror deciding if he should find someone "Not Guilty" for actually having violated an unjust law:

"If obedience to the established law be the
highest virtue, then the Patriots and Pilgrims of
New England, the Reformers of the Church, the
glorious company of the Apostles, the goodly
fellowship of the prophets, and the noble array
of martyrs, nay Jesus himself, were only
criminals and traitors."

He further said that when we permit disobedience to
one law, we need not fear destruction of all of our laws:

"Who is it that oppose the fugitive slave law?
Men that have always been on the side of law
and order and do not violate the statutes of man
for their own advantage. This disobedience to
the fugitive slave law is one of the strongest
guarantees for the observance of any just law.
You can not trust a people who will keep a law
because it is a law, nor dare we distrust a people
who will keep a law when it is just."

As cases involving the Fugitive Slave Act began their
long process through the courts, a curious thing happened. Juries hearing the cases of people who had violated the Act began issuing verdicts of "Not Guilty"

Since the people who were accused of violating this
law had been indicted by grand juries, the comments in
this book also apply to those who are called to serve on
grand juries. You should not permit yourself to be a
rubber stamp for some prosecutor who prides himself in
having successfully "sold" jurors through high pressure
techniques.

Most federal juries are composed of people who are
employees or spouses of employees of large corporations.
They take pride in being part of a system that they feel is
good. In order to preserve relationships with their friends
or employer, they have a tendency to go along with any
argument the government offers without giving it too
much thought. The history book is full of instances where

"good" people unquestioningly followed the "just" law of the land to their own destruction. In most instances, they knew the truth and what was going on, but would not lift one finger to help their fellow man. Their country, their precious personal security and their way of life were accordingly destroyed.

A number of other people commented on the Fugitive Slave Act, saying it was a bad law that should not be obeyed. These commentators went so far as to say that people should not be punished for violating this bad law.

A member of the House of Representatives said:

> "The spirit which threw the tea into Boston Harbor will set your infamous law at defiance. The spirit which overthrew the power of the British crown will submit to no force that shall constrain them to comply with the odious provisions of this enactment."

Various judges also publicly agreed with the concept that laws exist which should not be obeyed. In Vermont, Judge Theophilus Harrington stated: "The only evidence of ownership of a slave that I will accept is a bill of sale from God Almighty." Judge Benjamin Wade of Ohio insisted that he would never find someone guilty of violating the Fugitive Slave Act.

In your deliberations as a juror or grand juror, you should make sure that your decision is based upon your understanding of the facts and the law. If you do not understand the facts, or if you do not understand the law, then your decision should be "Not Guilty." It should also be "Not Guilty" if you feel that the law is unjust. The Fugitive Slave Act is a perfect illustration of this principle.

In another case, a defendant had been accused of mail fraud. He had neither money nor a lawyer to represent him. When it came time to decide if he wanted to be tried by a jury, he said, "No." He was summarily convicted. This conviction was overturned because the assistance of an attorney is necessary to make such an important decision which has a direct impact upon someone's liberty.[44]

**A jury may find a defendant "Not Guilty" even if the evidence of guilt is overwhelming or conclusive. A defendant may not be deprived of this right.[45]**

The Louisiana Supreme Court upheld a conviction of a defendant convicted of simple assault (placing someone in fear of being physically injured, but without actually touching them). The court stated that he was not entitled to a jury trial because the Louisiana law permitted jury trials only in cases where capital punishment or imprisonment at hard labor could be imposed. The U.S. Supreme Court reversed the decision. This case is interesting because it helps explain the duties of the jury:

"It is sufficient for present purposes to say that by the time our Constitution was written, jury trial in criminal cases had been in existence in England for several centuries and carried impressive credentials traced by many to Magna Carta. Its preservation and proper operation as a protection against arbitrary rule were among the major objectives of the revolutionary settlement which was expressed in the Declaration and Bill of Rights of 1689. In the 18th century, Blackstone could write, 'Our law has therefore wisely placed this strong and two-fold barrier, of a presentment and a trial by jury, between the liberties of the people and the prerogatives of the crown. It was necessary, for preserving the admirable balance of our constitution, to vest the executive power of the laws in the prince: and yet this power might be dangerous and destructive to that very constitution, if exerted without check or control, by justice oyer and terminer occasionally named by the crown; who might then, as in France or Turkey, imprison, dispatch, or exile any man that was obnoxious to the government, by an instant declaration that such is their will and pleasure. But the founders of the English law have, with excellent forecast, contrived that . . . the truth of every accusation, whether preferred in the shape of indictment, information, or appeal, should afterwards be confirmed by the unanimous suffrage of twelve of his equals and neighbours, indifferently chosen and superior to all suspicion.'"[46]

The concept of trial by jury came to America from England. Because the English government was interfering with juries in the 1770's, the American revolutionaries

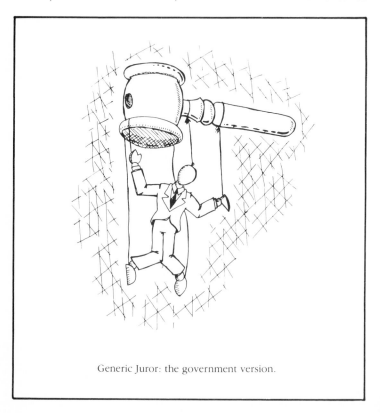

Generic Juror: the government version.

placed great importance on solving the problems created by an unjust jury system:

> "The guarantees of a jury trial in the Federal and State Constitutions reflect a profound judgment about the way in which law should be enforced and justice administered. A right to jury trial is granted to criminal defendants in order to prevent oppression by the government. Providing an accused with the right to be tried by a jury of his peers gave him an inestimable safeguard against the corrupt or overzealous prosecutor and against the compliant, biased, or eccentric judge. If the defendant preferred the common-sense judgment of a jury to the more tutored but perhaps less sympathetic reaction of the single judge, he was to have it. Beyond this, the jury trial provisions in the Federal and State Constitutions reflect a fundamental decision about the exercise of official power - - a reluctance to entrust plenary powers over the life and liberty of the citizen to one judge or to a group of judges. Fear of unchecked power, so typical of our State and Federal Governments in other respects, found expression in the criminal law in this insistence upon community participation in the determination of guilt or innocence. The deep commitment of the Nation to the right of jury trial in serious criminal cases as a defense against arbitrary law enforcement qualifies for protection under the Due Process Clause of the Fourteenth Amendment, and must therefore be respected by the States."[47]

In civil trials where the evidence is sufficiently one-sided, the judge may attempt to order the jury to issue a verdict against a party. In criminal cases, the judge cannot do this. The jury must be free from direct control in its verdict. This means that the jury must also be free from judicial pressure:

> "It is one of the most essential features of the right of trial by jury that no jury should be compelled to find any but a general verdict in criminal cases, and the removal of this safeguard would violate its design and destroy its spirit. A general verdict is a simple statement: 'Guilty or Not Guilty.'"[48]

But the matter is more subtle and goes further than that with many judges. When a judge asks the jury to answer special questions in its decision-making process, it creates in the mind of the juror an erroneous impression that he has to justify whatever decision he makes to the judge.

Justice Black and Justice Douglas of the U.S. Supreme Court described this abuse by judges who issue long lists of questions for the jury to answer, instead of having the jury arrive at a "Guilty or Not Guilty" verdict:

> "Such devices are used to impair or wholly take away the power of a jury to render a general verdict. One of the ancient, fundamental reasons for having general jury verdicts was to preserve the right of trial by jury as an indispensable part of a free government. Many of the most famous constitutional controversies in England revolved around litigants' insistence, particularly in seditious libel cases (cases involving people who speak out against the government), that a jury had the right to render a general verdict without being compelled to return a number of subsidiary findings to support its general verdict. Some English jurors had to go to jail because they insisted upon their right to render general verdicts over the repeated command of tyrannical judges not to do so.' Justices Black and Douglas concluded their decision by saying this practice 'is but another means uti-

lized by courts to weaken the constitutional power of juries and to vest judges with more power to decide cases according to their own judgments."[49]

The Supreme Court overturned the conviction of Dr. Spock, an outspoken critic of the Vietnam War and world famous for his books on child raising. What about the jurors who found him guilty? They were the ones who caused his enormous pain and expense. Dr. Spock had to defend his own constitutional rights, since the jurors obviously didn't care about these rights.

You can read about that jury in a very thoughtful book by Jessica Mitford, entitled The Trial of Dr. Spock, published by Alfred A. Knopf, New York, 1969. Mrs. Mitford made a study of the entire trial, including the jury.[50]

These jurors were cowards in our society, people without souls whose claim to existence was that they were efficient parasites on the framework of our Bill of Rights. They sought its benefits, but were unwilling to defend the Bill of Rights from the tyrants who proliferate in our bureaucracy.

Those horrible scoundrels spent their free time as jurors whining about being away from their families and jobs. They were overwhelmed with the authority figures (the U.S. Marshals) who cared for them. They were filled with compassion at the nervousness of the Draft Board clerk. Yet none of them was willing to support the concept of freedom of speech contained in our Bill of Rights.

The most shocking act that they committed as jurors, in their dishonor of the decision-making process, was revealed when they were asked whether they agreed with the anti-war activities of Dr. Spock. Apparently some of them agreed with him and with what he was attempting to do regarding the war in Vietnam. However, they thought that because he did break the law, they had no choice but to find him guilty.

There is no question about it. The jurors did not know what their rights were. They found Dr. Spock guilty, and violated their own consciences and codes of what is right and wrong.

Had the jurors in the Dr. Spock case been loyal, patriotic Americans, citizens who knew what their rights were, they would have found him "Not Guilty," and by doing so would have vetoed or nullified a law that they found repugnant. But no one had told them about their rights.

If you do not know your rights, you have none. You must find out, on your own, what your rights are. You cannot rely upon others to protect your rights. The government certainly has never been interested in anything other than controlling you. If you want to be a good juror, you are going to have to break out of the corral of your ignorance so that you will not be in the category of the whining juror who sincerely regrets making a bad decision. Not knowing one's rights is an insufficient excuse for a bad decision. No one told Dr. Spock's jurors what their rights were. Are we to be left with nothing more than the impression that we all must stand in a long line and sincerely forgive those poor, ignorant jurors for being stains on the rights of man?

In another case, a defendant had refused to be inducted into the Army during the Vietnam War. The judge was so infuriated by the defendant's conduct that he refused him the right to trial by jury. The proceedings continued to a final conviction, but this decision was overturned because we all have a right to a jury trial.[51]

In a similar case, the judge told the jury:

> "I, therefore instruct you it is your duty as jurors to return a verdict of guilty. You may consider this matter and you may disregard my instructions, but I am instructing you as a matter of law that it is your duty to return a verdict of guilty as charged in the indictment."[52]

40

"Your family was hungry? My family is hungry all the time, but *I* don't steal!"

Those jurors, being very weak and impressed by the judge, totally disregarded their duty as jurors and found the defendant guilty. The case was overturned because **a trial judge may not direct a verdict of guilty in a criminal case**. The jury should have refused to convict the defendant, but did not. Perhaps those jurors wanted to impress their friends after the trial. Perhaps they were grossly ignorant or cared nothing about their own liberty. Regardless of their reasoning or lack of it, they did wrong, and the defendant was permanently injured.

There are three verdicts a jury may issue:

   (a)  **Guilty**
   (b)  **Not Guilty**
   (c)  **Hung Jury (deadlocked)**

When a jury is deadlocked because a few people on the jury do not agree with the majority, the judge may call the jurors before him and read to them something called a *dynamite* or *Allen* charge. This specially prepared statement will hypnotize, induce or convince the jurors in the minority to change their minds, to go along with the majority, even if they don't want to because they feel that the person accused is not guilty. That actually happened in a case where one juror told the others that if they voted "Not Guilty," the judge would "get all over those that voted not guilty."

Here is what the judge told the jurors in order to get them to change their minds and to find the accused guilty. It is very long and boring, but you are going to be shocked when you finish reading it:

"Mr. Foreman, and members of the jury, the Court has received the information that you sent me from the standpoint of your having been, right before the lunch hour, at that time unable to reach a verdict.

"I have asked you to come back in here to talk with you a little further. You have been in your jury room in the process of deliberating for approximately overall, sixteen hours. In view of the time consumed, and the evidence, and particularly documentary evidence, that is not unusual.

"However, I wish to make a few suggestions, which you may desire to consider in your deliberations, along with all the evidence and all the instructions previously given.

"This, as you well realize, is an important case. The trial has been expensive to both the prosecution and the defense. If you should fail to agree on a verdict, the case is left open and undecided. Like all cases, it must be disposed of sometime. There appears no reason to believe that another trial would not be equally expensive to both sides. Nor does there appear any reason to believe that the case can be tried again better or more exhaustively than it has been, on either side. Any further jury must be selected in the same manner and from the same source as you have been chosen. So there appears no reason to believe that the case would ever be submitted to twelve men and women more intelligent, more impartial, or more competent to decide it, or that more or clearer evidence could be produced on behalf of either side.

"Of course these matters suggest themselves upon brief reflection to all of us who have sat through this trial. The only reason they are mentioned is because some of them may have escaped your attention, which must have been fully occupied up to this time in reviewing the evidence. They are matters which, along with others and perhaps more obvious ones, remind us how important and desirable it is that you unanimously agree upon a verdict of "Guilty" or "Not Guilty," if you can do so without violence to your own individual judgment and conscience.

"It is unnecessary to add that the Court does not wish any juror to surrender his or her conscientious convictions. As stated in the instructions given at the time the case was submitted to you, do not surrender your honest convictions as to the weight or effect of evidence solely because of the opinion of the other jurors, or for the mere purpose of returning a verdict.

"However, it is your duty as jurors to consult with one another and to deliberate with a view to reaching an agreement, if you can do so without violence to individual judgment. Each of you must decide the case for yourself, but

43

The Golden Ruling: He who has the gold gets the ruling.

you should do so only after a consideration of the evidence with your fellow jurors. And in the course of your deliberations, you should not hesitate to change your opinion when convinced it is erroneous.

"In order to bring twelve minds to an unanimous result, you must examine the questions submitted to you with candor and frankness, and with proper deference to and regard for the opinions of each other. That is to say, in conferring together, each of you should pay due attention and respect to the views of the others, and listen to each other's arguments with a disposition to re-examine your own views.

"If much the greater of you are for a conviction, each dissenting juror ought to consider whether a doubt in his or her own mind is a reasonable one, since it makes no effective impression upon the minds of so many equally honest, equally intelligent fellow jurors, who bear the same responsibility, serve under the sanction of the same oath, and have heard the same evidence with, we may assume, the same attention and a equal desire to arrive at the truth. On the other hand, if a majority or even a lesser number of you are for acquittal, other jurors ought to seriously ask themselves again whether they do not have a reason to doubt the correctness of a judgment which is not concurred in by many of their fellow jurors, and whether they should not distrust the weight or sufficiency of evidence which fails to convince the minds of several of their fellows to a moral certainty and beyond a reasonable doubt.

"You are not partisans. You've got no friends to reward; no enemies to punish. You are judges — judges of the facts. Your sole purpose is to ascertain the truth from the evidence before you. You are the sole and exclusive judges of the credibility of all of the witnesses and the weight and effect of all the evidence. In the performance of this high duty, you are at liberty to disregard all comments of both court and counsel, including of course the remarks I am now making to you.

"Remember at all times that no juror is expected to yield a conscientious conviction he or she may have as to the weight or effect of evidence. But remember also that, after full deliberation and consideration of all the evidence, it is your duty to agree upon a verdict, if

45

you can do so without violating your individual judgment and your individual conscience.

"You may conduct your deliberations as you choose, but I suggest, however, that when you retire you carefully re-examine and reconsider all the evidence bearing upon the questions before you.

"Under these instructions, since there are multiple defendants charged in this indictment, you may find one or more of the accused guilty or not guilty as charged in the indictment. And at any time during your deliberations you may return into court your verdict of guilty or not guilty with respect to any defendant charged and on trial, as to whom you have unanimously agreed upon a verdict as to any of the defendants charged or on trial in this indictment.

"You may be as leisurely in your deliberations as the occasion requires; and you shall take all the time which you may feel is necessary. The marshals have been instructed, and are now instructed, to take you to your hotel whenever you are ready to go.

"You may now retire, Mr. Foreman, and members of the jury and continue your deliberations in such manner as shall be determined by your good and conscientious judgment as reasonable men and women."[53]

Well now! That sounded like a reasonable explanation, except for the fact that the judge is ignoring the verdict that the jury has issued: it is a deadlocked (hung) jury.

Let me reveal a few more of the facts: 1) Two of the jurors wanted to go home. They were insisting upon it. They were the ones voting "Not Guilty." 2) It was Labor Day Weekend. The jurors could have been as leisurely as they wanted about making their decision. They could have stayed there for another week or two, but then they would not spend the Labor Day holiday with their loved ones. 3) The judge was getting paid a substantial salary, so he did not have to worry about suffering any loss of money if the jury wanted to continue debating the case for days. 4) The attorneys were getting paid large sums of money for participating in the trial. 5) The jurors, on the other hand, were getting paid next to nothing because *their real payment was in doing their civic duty.* The jury was "leisurely" making its decision, and the jurors could go home when they voted as the judge wanted them to, whenever that might be.

Do you think that the verdict of "Guilty," rendered 90 minutes later in this case, indicated that the jurors really thought someone was guilty, or do you think they just went ahead and made the easiest decision possible so they could go home to have a beer and watch the football game?

My opinion of their decision is that they simply arrived at the following conclusion: "I don't care who is convicted or who goes to jail. The defendants can go to hell. I have better things to do than to sit here wasting my time."

What would you have done? Would you have disregarded the rights and liberties of the accused defendants? If you are ever on trial, do you want your jury to be concerned more about your rights or about hurrying home to watch a football game?

Judge John Brown explained the same problem in one of his opinions:

> "The jury was subjected to appeals and pressures which had nothing to do with innocence or guilt of the defendant on trial. A conscientious citizen serving as a juror wants earnestly to do his duty. He is impressed, as he should be, by the awesome power and prestige of a United States Judge. In performing his role in the pursuit of justice, the juror wants to feel that he is as

47

loyal, as conscientious, as fearless, as courageous and as objective as the judge. He wants to
be a good citizen. He desires, for at least this
one time in his life, to measure up to what he
senses and feels in the atmosphere of the courtroom. He is told by the judge that it is wasteful
of the judge's time, the taxpayers' money, and
interferes with the rights of others to secure trial
and the services of attorneys if the case must be
retried. He is told that a decision must be made
and that it might as well be made now.

"This is not a free jury. Done with more
finesse and sophistication, the practical effect of
the charge is the same as the now historically
discredited coercive power of the judge over

"If you don't hurry up and vote guilty, I'll miss the
football game!"

the jury when its verdict displeased the judge. The strength of the jury system is its absolute, real, actual independence. It must take its instruction on the law from the judge, but the jury alone determines the facts. It is simply not legally correct that some jury must sometime decide that the defendant is 'Guilty' or 'Not Guilty.' The fact is, as history reminds us, a succession of juries may legitimately fail to agree until, at long last, the prosecution gives up. But such juries, perhaps more courageous than any other, have performed their useful, vital function in our system. This is the kind of independence which should be encouraged. It is in this independence that liberty is secured.

"In many phases of criminal law we have come a long, long way since 1896. There is no longer any place for the 'Allen' charge. For good reasons it has acquired its descriptive as the 'dynamite' charge (variously called the 'nitro-glycerin' charge) at the hands of the Bar. This is an intrusion by the judge into the exclusive domain of fact-finding by the jury. It is not any less an intrusion, merely because the judge does not indicate which of two decisions must be reached.

"What is worse, it is becoming more and more commonplace. Nearly every hard-fought criminal case coming to this Court reveals the judge sooner or later giving this charge or some embellishment of it. Too often, as in these two cases, it was but a matter of a few hours after the jury had retired to deliberate. Not infrequently, as we were led to believe on oral argument in both of these cases, it occurs with the last jury in the last case at that division point for that particular term. To the other pressures which are irrelevant is the other and natural one of a personal consideration for the judge who, like the jurors, also wants to go home. The charge pointedly reminds them that to hold out disrupts the plans of all.

"I think a mistrial from a hung jury is a safeguard to liberty. In many areas it is the sole means by which one or a few may stand out against an overwhelming contemporary public sentiment. Nothing should interfere with its exercise. In the final analysis the 'Allen' charge itself does not make sense. All it may rightfully say is that there is a duty to consider the views of others but that a conscientious person has finally the right to stand by conscience. If it says that and nothing more it is a superfluous lecture in citizenship. If it says more to declare that there is a duty to decide, it is legally incorrect as an interference with that rightful independence.

"The time has come, I think, to forbid this practice. Like the silver platter, this is too dear to keep. The cost in fundamental fairness is too great."[54]

# The Other Side of the Coin

Not every judge is unethical or prejudiced in favor of the government. Just as a judge can be good or bad, so can a juror be good or bad. Anarchy, whether it be the anarchy of the judiciary or the anarchy of the jury, is totally unacceptable if we are going to have a legal system that actually represents liberty and justice.

Remember the terrible event of December 7, 1941 — Japan's attack on Pearl Harbor. Soon thereafter, all people of Japanese ancestry in the United States were threatened with arrest by the federal government and placed in concentration camps.

For all practical purposes, their property was confiscated. They were dispossessed of their homes. They were subjected to the same trauma we all lament when it happens in a country we have classified as a dictatorship.

These people of Japanese ancestry had committed no crimes against the United States. The theft of their property and their imprisonment by the government of the United States was accomplished by the president's executive orders.

Mr. Korematsu was one of those Japanese persons. He refused to go to the concentration camp, as I am sure any

51

logical-thinking person would be inclined to react. He was convicted in Federal District Court for not going to the concentration camp.

His loyalty was never even questioned and, in fact, he was extremely loyal to the United States. However, the U.S. Supreme Court upheld his conviction.

Let's briefly examine the dissenting opinions of the three justices. Justice Roberts:

"..., it is the case of convicting a citizen as a punishment for not submitting to imprisonment in a concentration camp, based on his ancestry, and solely because of his ancestry, without evidence or inquiry concerning his loyalty and good disposition towards the United States. If this be a correct statement of the facts disclosed by the record, and facts of which we take judicial notice, I need hardly labor the conclusion that Constitutional rights have been violated."

Justice Murphy:

"Justification for the exclusion (concentration camps) is sought, instead, mainly upon questionable racial and sociological grounds . . . I dissent, therefore, from this legalization of racism. Racial discrimination in any form and in any degree has no justifiable part whatever in our democratic way of life. It is unattractive in any setting but it is utterly revolting among a free people who have embraced the principles set forth in the Constitution of the United States. All residents of this nation are kin in some way by blood or culture to a foreign land. Yet they are primarily and necessarily a part of the new and distinct civilization of the United States. They must accordingly be treated at all times as the heirs of the American experiment and as entitled to all the rights and freedoms guaranteed by the Constitution."

Justice Jackson:

"But here is an attempt to make an otherwise innocent act a crime merely because this prisoner is the son of parents as to whom he had no choice, and belongs to a race from which there is no way to resign."[55]

But those comments were from justices who were in the minority. Korematsu was convicted.

The excuse given for this act of tyranny was that in

Korematsu's crime: Wrong ancestry, wrong race, wrong religion.

wartime it is more important to safeguard the nation than to be concerned with the rights of the people. But safeguard who from what? Not one of the people of Japanese ancestry placed in the United States Concentration Camp System was an enemy of the United States, nor was any of them a spy. They were merely loyal Americans.

So, had *YOU* been on that jury shortly after the attack on Pearl Harbor before which the crime of refusing to go to a concentration camp was being tried, would you have been in favor of placing the people of Japanese ancestry in concentration camps and confiscating their property?

Probably no one asked you for your opinion. But they did ask the courts, which said that the concentration camps and the mass confiscation of property that ensued were just fine.

Instead of people of Japanese ancestry, would you have voted for a conviction had the accused been of:
a) Jewish ancestry,
b) Mexican ancestry,
c) German ancestry,
d) Black ancestry,
e) Baptist background,
f) Catholic background,
g) Presbyterian background?

The matter of ancestry and religion is relevant because ethnic background was not the only issue here. The non-Christian religious background of the accused, Mr. Korematsu, was also considered as evidence against him.

In this case and numerous others the lesson is clear. Ultimately, jurors should examine their individual consciences to determine if they should even be jurors in the first place.

# Should YOU Be A Juror?

When our representatives sit in deliberation in Washington and vote on new laws, they produce laws based upon many compromises. Powerful special interest groups such as the banking and petroleum empires have an impressive ability, due to their incredible wealth, to actually have laws written with their organizational goals in mind. You, the average citizen, cannot participate in this process of legislation.

So laws are passed, whether good or bad, efficient or inefficient. If there is too great a difference of opinion as to what a law should contain, then the time is not right to pass such a law. If passed under such divisive conditions, the law will probably be bad or inefficient, or both. Further, laws that are thrown together as a result of public outcry cannot be good or efficient because of the passionate conditions under which they are created.

As a juror, you are being asked to consider whether a law, as applied to an alleged violator of that law, is good or bad. Your vote as to the innocence or guilt of the accused will determine whether the government will continue to use that law as a basis to seek conviction of its violators.

If that law is fair and just as it applies to the accused, after you examine and understand the facts of the case, then the accused may be found guilty. If the law is neither fair nor just, then you, the juror, can "veto" it by finding the accused "Not Guilty," as no one can be guilty of violating an unjust law.

The laws that our representatives pass for us to obey are not sacred. Many times laws are wrong. The Fugitive Slave Act was a bad law, as were the laws forbidding blacks to eat in restaurants or to sit in the front of buses.

Once a law is passed, we have the duty and obligation to decide whether it should be obeyed. Does the law assist in promoting "life, liberty and the pursuit of happiness," or does it impinge upon our lives, erase our liberty and cancel our pursuit of happiness?

Obviously, to be a good juror requires not only the basic intelligence of the common working man or woman, it also requires that traditional strength of character and appreciation of fairness for which this nation is famous.

If you fear the judge, or you are afraid you will be fired from your job if you make the wrong decision, tell the judge.

If you feel the judge is involved in some kind of conspiracy to convict an innocent person, tell the judge as well as the defense attorney.

If you feel that your personality is so inadequate that you worship the authority of the state, and you feel the state is never wrong, tell the judge as well as the defense attorney.

Ask the court to excuse you from being a juror, but be honest about your reasons. It is really very evil for you to be a "yes man" or "rubber stamp" of the government and at the same time a member of the jury. There are many people whose "god" is the government. Naturally, you cannot be an honest juror if that is your belief. In that case, you should tell the judge of your problem, asking to be released as a juror.

Being fair is not the same thing as fraudulently participating in a procedure that is generally fair. If you are an unfair, biased, selfish, short-sighted person, your mere presence in the jury makes the procedure unfair and useless. Persons who benefit from our societal practices, based upon the Bill of Rights, and are unwilling to defend those rights by being fair and unbiased jurors, are neither religious nor ethical people. They may put on a facade of being religious as they parade to church on Sunday to show off their fashionable clothing but they are not ethical. They are not supporting the Bill of Rights.

If you are such a person, simply tell the judge that you have no character; that you will not make an independent decision because you fear making any decision that would upset anyone.

Famous Colonial Violators of British Law
Would you convict them?

If the judge refuses to listen, stand up in open court and ask that you be released as a juror because you will probably vote for the conviction of the accused. If you cannot be honest about anything else in your life, at least be honest this one time. Your social unfairness among your acquaintances is of little value or importance to anyone. You are going to be in the position of destroying someone's life if you don't speak up and confess to the judge that you are a coward without any moral values, unwilling to consider as true anything other than what the government or the multinational corporation wants you to believe.

Comparison is another way of discerning whether you should be a juror. You no doubt feel that you are a good citizen. Well then, were George Washington and Thomas Jefferson good English citizens? Do you look up to them and revere their memory as great men?

They were good citizens — probably just like you would like to be — but they did not like the oppressive laws of England. They began a violent, bloody revolution against their country's laws, *and we all won!*

The only good citizen is the one who is distrustful and suspicious of his government. Not that any other governmental system is better than ours. None is. But we all know how shady our politicians can be and always have been. It is a common opinion that whenever a politician makes a statement, he is probably lying. If it happens that he didn't lie, then the witness to that event, at that instant, just witnessed a bona fide miracle.

The actual responsibility for the execution of our nation's laws rests upon the shoulders of the jurors, who must decide if the manner in which a law is to be applied is fair and just.

Are you willing to assert your rights and maybe even risk going to jail, as other good and faithful citizens have done for hundreds of years to force the government to conduct fair jury trials? If your answer is "Yes," you can be an honest juror; if your answer is "No," you cannot.

There are important factors for you to consider in answering the inquiry into whether you should even be a juror. Most people receive a jury service notification in the mail. They appear and may or may not be selected. When they are selected, they are usually silent as to what they really believe because they have no information upon which to make a decision, either good or bad. They tend to want to make a decision that will not offend the judge or the government.

Of course, that is an extremely dishonest attitude toward the trial of alleged offenders. That is why if you have doubts about whether you have the ability to be a fair, impartial juror, you should tell the judge. If the judge is hostile, then tell the defense attorney. If neither of them shows interest in your dilemma, file a complaint in the form of a letter against the attorney and address it to the bar association of your state. Also, file a complaint in letter form against the judge with the judicial qualifications board of your state.

You probably won't have to go that far in your search for justice, but it is nice to know that such procedures do exist.

Now, you may ask yourself, "If I am such a coward, how will I be able to assert myself in this manner?" Obviously, if you can go through with this procedure, you are not as much of a coward as one would think, although not being able to be a fair and impartial juror is certainly a sad commentary on your life. By being honest about your weakness, you will not commit a crime against your fellow man. Pretending to be fair and impartial, but in your heart knowing that you are the opposite, is a horrible crime.

Here are some hypothetical situations so you can ascertain your suitability as a fair and impartial juror:

### Example A

It is illegal to help slaves escape from the South. It is illegal to give them food, hide them, or help them in any way. Various federal laws of the United States provide for fines and imprisonment for anyone violating these laws. You are a juror in a trial where someone has been accused of such an offense. All of the evidence shows that the accused did, in fact, help some slaves who escaped from the South by giving them food, clothing and shelter.

You have taken an oath as a juror to follow the law as presented to you by the judge. The judge has given you instructions which, if followed, will result in a verdict of guilty. The jury foreman works for a large oil company, and he has been very rude with the jurors, insisting that anyone who violates any law should be punished. Every one of the jurors agrees with the jury foreman except you. They all want to go home. They are bored. So, how are you going to vote?

If you are an honest juror in this example, you will disregard anything the judge has told you and vote according to your conscience. No law can force you to commit a crime against what you feel is right or wrong. In this matter, you should vote "Not Guilty." A law that requires you to do evil ceases being a law the moment it requires you to commit an act you feel is sinful.

On the other hand, if you voted "Guilty," knowing you did not really believe that the law was just or that the accused should be punished, you have injured an innocent person and damaged the jury system by making a joke of it, and you will forever have to live with the bad decision you made. You should not have been a juror.

## Example B

It is illegal to refuse to be inducted into the Army. There is a criminal penalty for refusing to be drafted and you have been selected as a juror in such a case. The attorney for the accused wants to ask the jurors questions, but the judge keeps refusing to let him ask any questions. The jury foreman works for a company that makes ammunition. He has made a few harsh comments to the other jurors about "draft dodgers."

During the trial, the judge refuses to let the attorney introduce evidence regarding the constitutional illegality of undeclared wars. Throughout the trial this judge is hostile to the defense attorney but permits the prosecution to do anything it desires. In the instructions to the jurors, he explains that they have sworn under oath to follow the law as he has presented it to them.

On the other hand, you feel that the law is unfair. The war is illegal because it is an undeclared war. You also feel that the judge is biased and has been grossly unfair to the accused.

You also feel that if you vote "Not Guilty" you may lose your job. You don't really know that for a fact, but you are afraid to do anything that would upset the judge or the prosecutor. You normally feel that the laws are good and that anyone accused of violating them should be convicted if the evidence proves guilt, except now. Your conscience really troubles you.

Under these circumstances you, the juror, have the opportunity to "veto" a bad law. If you are afraid to make an honest decision you should explain, either to the judge or to the defense attorney, that you are afraid to make a decision in the matter.

If you go ahead and disregard your sincerely held notions of right and wrong to convict a person only because the government wants you to, you should not have been on the jury.

### *Example C*

You have been selected to be a juror in a tax case. You have heard stories about how the tax authorities investigate people who criticize them in any way. Now you are going to be the decision-maker in one of those cases. But you don't want to get investigated. After all, you have worked hard to have a house and a car, and you don't want the tax authorities to take your house and car away from you and throw you and your family out into the street. You have also heard about how they can take anyone's tax return, find mistakes on it, then have that person convicted and sent to jail. In short, you are scared to death that if you make the wrong decision in the case you may get harassed by the tax authorities.

The jury foreman is a retired government employee and has made statements to the effect that taxes help pay for his retirement. During the deliberations, it has become apparent to the other jurors that you really don't want to make a decision. You haven't paid too much attention to the trial at all. You saw people talking during the trial, but you didn't understand because you kept thinking about what would happen to you and your poor family if you made a decision that angered the government. After all, the taxing authorities can find out anything about anyone and use that information to send them to jail.

It is obvious that you should not have been selected as a juror. You should tell the judge and the defense attorney about your fears. But you should not make a decision regarding the guilt or innocence of the accused. To do so would be an incredible fraud upon the nation's court system.

Obviously, you are more devoted to your few humble possessions than you are to your own rights. This also means that you couldn't care less about the rights of others.

If you cannot convince the judge to release you as a juror, then the only way out of the problem is to either vote "Guilty" or "Not Guilty."

You cannot honestly vote "Guilty" because you didn't understand the case. If you vote "Not Guilty," you fear that the tax man will begin harassing you.

You are in this dilemma because you failed to explain to the court at the outset about your fears and lack of courage. Any decision you make at this point is going to be wrong. However, if you vote "Guilty," someone is going to go to jail. Under that vote, you would be helping to convict someone based upon your uneducated guess. In this situation, you will do the least damage by voting "Not Guilty."

### Example D

The federal government has taken control of the curriculum of public schools. Many members of various religious denominations have begun removing their children from public schools. It has become a national problem because the public is repudiating the concept of public schools. Some children are being placed in private schools, but larger numbers are being enrolled in home-study programs and attending school at home.

Congress passes a law making it a criminal offense for parents to refuse to send their children to public schools. Although private schools are permitted, home study is ignored as an option. The federal government begins to arrest parents who teach their children at home. A special provision of the law requires all parents who are teaching their children at home to present themselves for detention if their children are not enrolled in public schools by a certain date. The parents are detained in areas such as sports arenas while special concentration camps are prepared for them. Their children are placed in foster homes and are not allowed to communicate with their parents.

You have been selected as a juror in such a case involving a mother and a father who refused to send their child to a public school. These parents also refused to present themselves for imprisonment in a concentration camp.

The law mandates that the parents must present themselves for imprisonment if they are refusing to send their children to public schools. The law specifies as punishment a fine of $50,000, imprisonment for not more than twenty years, and the placement of the child in a special government foster home where the child will be re-educated to forget about his criminal parents.

The parents are too poor to have an attorney represent them. They object to the court-appointed attorney because he wants them to plead guilty, so they represent themselves. The

64

judge is very disrespectful toward them. He doesn't permit them to present any evidence. The prosecutor presents his case in an orderly and professional manner and definitely proves that the mother and father are guilty of violating the law. Should you find the parents guilty or not guilty?

You should find the parents "Not Guilty" because the law is repugnant to the Constitution. But you should also arrive at that same verdict because the parents have not been permitted to have a trial. When the judge refuses to permit lay persons to present their own cases, and when he refuses to guide them through the tangle of procedures, the judge has denied them a trial.

In these examples, involving fugitive slaves, draft resisters, tax evaders and noncompliance with compulsory education, the juror should vote "Not Guilty." This verdict should be given even though the accused is clearly in violation of the letter of the law. The moral and ethical responsibility of the juror is to determine whether a law is just.

# Jury
# Selection

The word *jury* refers to the twelve, or sometimes six, people who are selected to hear the evidence and decide guilt or innocence in a trial.

The term *venire* is the abbreviated form of the Latin phrase *venire facias juratores*. Venire refers to the writ directed to an official, usually the sheriff, to require a certain number of people to appear in court to serve as jurors.

Another common word used in discussing the jury is *panel*. This word can be used to describe the group of people from which the jury is selected, or it can mean the group of people that is actually going to be the jury.

*Juror* can mean either a person selected to serve on a jury or one of the persons chosen from the group from which the jury will be selected.

*Talesmen* are those people summoned to appear when there is a deficiency in the number of the jurors chosen to sit as the jury.

Jurors are usually selected from various public lists, such as voter registration lists, driver's license lists, telephone directories and utility company customer lists. Use of a single list such as a voter registration list results in excluding people 18 to 34 years of age, Spanish-surnamed people, blacks, people with four years or less of education, laborers and women.[56]

Many people are exempted by statute from service on the jury. People over 65 years of age, employees of the state or the United States, ministers of the gospel, physicians, dentists, attorneys and spouses of attorneys, firefighters, certain railroad employees, members of the national guard on active duty, women who have children under sixteen years of age, nurses, practitioners of faith healing, morticians, pharmacists, forestry workers, school teachers, and spouses of people who are on the same jury may be exempted from jury service by state law. Of course, the exempted classifications vary from state to state.

However, if one of those persons exempted wants to serve on the jury, he may do so. The exemption must be asserted by the person himself if he does not want to serve on the jury.

It is common for a state law to provide that people who cannot see, hear or feel are excluded from juries. This means that blind, deaf, and partially paralyzed people are discriminated against because of their physical condition. They are second-class citizens in states with such laws.

Each juror is paid a certain amount for his services. This is usually a minimal amount of money that is certainly not realistic. If the jury has to be present overnight, the government has to pay for the food and lodging.

There is one detail you should be aware of as you begin your experience as a juror. If the case that you will hear involves the federal or state government or a multinational corporation, investigators for those organizations will have already begun an investigation of you. The investigation includes data such as birth records, political involvement, trade or profession, tax records, credit rating, ownership of real and personal property, medical information, matters concerning relatives and neighbors, racial background, personal prejudices, and sexual behavior.

This information helps those organizations choose the type of juror whom they feel will aid in the successful prosecution of their case. Under these circumstances it is not very complimentary for you to be selected as a juror. The attorneys for those organizations have decided that it will be relatively simple to influence you to support their arguments. This means that they are certain that you are not very independent in your thoughts and are easily swayed by their position as authority figures in the community.

A topic of interest to the juror is how challenges to a particular person or perhaps to the entire group of jurors are handled. When a challenge is made, the juror or jurors may be found to be unacceptable and would then be released from jury duty.

If the attorney doing the examination does not like a prospective juror, he can exercise a *peremptory challenge.* The attorney, by statute, may use a certain limited number of peremptory challenges for which no explanation need be made. If you are challenged in this manner, you will be able to return home. There is no problem with this concept, because no one wants a prejudiced juror to sit in a trial. One limitation on this practice is that the state cannot use peremptory challenges based upon race to eliminate prospective jurors.

The other type of challenge is called the *challenge for cause.* To use this type of challenge, the attorney must to give a specific reason why a particular person should not serve as a juror. There are laws that outline what constitutes a cause for which a person should not be a juror. Generally we can say that if a person admits to a situation which would prejudice or bias the decision, then that person should not be a juror.

*Voir dire* is the term used to describe the practice of questioning prospective jurors. This is the preselection examination of the prospective juror to determine if he is a qualified, fair-minded person.

If the attorney asks each prospective juror questions concerning his ability to make fair and just decisions, the attorney is doing his job correctly. If he poses the questions to the group of jurors, at the same time and as a group, then he is not doing his job correctly, and the poor defendant is not receiving adequate representation by that attorney. Most likely that trial will not be a fair one and you, the juror, will have to be very careful in watching the events as they unfold.

In federal courts, the voir dire occurs in a different way. The questions that the attorney wants to ask of the jurors are submitted to the judge. The judge then asks the questions he chooses. Naturally, any fair-minded individual would conclude that under these conditions it is impossible to receive a fair trial in any federal court.

This is especially true if the trial is a "political trial" in which the government is trying to "get" someone because of that person's criticism of the government.

In these question-and-answer processes, the attorneys can make very broad statements in order to inform the juror of the case. From this point forward, and throughout the trial, things may be said that are improper if a fair trial is to take place. The judge may instruct you to "disregard the remark that was just made." Of course, this is dishonest in itself. How can you disregard a remark once you have heard it? If that happens more than once or twice during the trial, it means that the judge and/or the prosecutor is trying to force you to make a specific decision. They are interfering with your right as a juror to make a fair decision.

It is particularly important to ferret out matters of racial prejudice. If the person on trial is black and you do not like blacks for some reason, the accused cannot receive a fair trial at your hands. You should be excused from jury duty. Similarly, if you are a member of the black race who does not like whites, you should be excused as a juror because you cannot possibly make a fair decision.

Membership in certain organizations may make it doubtful that the person can come to a fair decision in a particular case. Membership in the "Klan," "law and order groups," the Knights of Pythias, Odd Fellows and Freemasons have been the topics of questions to prospective jurors in voir dire concerning the ability of a member of such an organization to make a fair decision in a trial.

Naturally, a person who is a friend of an accused or who is involved with the accused in business relationships should be excused from jury duty.

There are some religious groups whose membership will be excluded from jury duty. If the juror is a member of a religious group that opposes capital punishment, that person will be excused from jury service as will a member of a religious group that teaches that no man can judge another man. However, there are those who believe that excluding someone from a jury on religious grounds denies the accused a fair trial. They argue that the jury, without that person, does not represent a cross-section of the community.

In our society we unfortunately have large numbers of people who are "police statists." These people share the same social ideology as the Nazis in Germany prior to and during World War II. They believe that regardless of what the prosecutor or the police do, whether it is legal or illegal, ethical or unethical, it is good. They do not believe that you are innocent until proven guilty. They believe that if the state accuses you, you are guilty, and you cannot prove your innocence. Nor would they believe it even if the accused proved his innocence. These people are a cancer on a free society. They should not be permitted to be jurors; yet they often are. If these people are on the jury with you, you cannot vote in agreement with them without becoming an accomplice to tyranny.

You may not be allowed to be a juror if you do not like informers. An informer is a person who by treachery becomes a "friend" of someone in order to testify against him at a later date. He is usually paid for his "services" by the government. Such a person is often referred to as a stool pigeon, fink, or snitch. Many times the informer will actually initiate the planning of a crime and, through his friendship with the person he is working against, obtain the help of his "friend" in committing a crime. The "friend" will then be tried and convicted for this crime. The courts permit informers to testify. This activity is immoral and unethical, and if you rely on the word of an informer to find someone guilty, then you are no better than the informer.

Prospective jurors may not be accepted for jury service due to successful challenges to their participation on the jury. The attorney can use a fixed number of peremptory challenges. As explained above, no reason has to be given for the peremptory challenge.

You should also be aware of the process for selecting a jury foreman, particularly since the role of this jury member is of considerable concern. The foreman will be the spokesman for the jury. You should not, under any circumstances, accept an *authority figure* as the foreman. If the foreman is a police officer, government employee or an employee of a multi-national corporation (a corporation that operates in more than one country), he is not going to make a fair decision in the case. He will vote for the point of view of the government or corporation, regardless of the facts.

Furthermore, such a foreman has the ability to overwhelm normal working people by deceiving, mistreating, threatening, or yelling at them. And, as I mention throughout this book, such a foreman feels that he must vote in favor of the government; otherwise he may fail to receive another promotion, be blacklisted, or even lose his job.

The theory behind trial by jury is that unbiased, unprejudiced people listening to all of the testimony can make a fair and just decision. Whether this actually happens is merely philosophical speculation. A more realistic impression is that trials are used to validate (make an official act appear legal) whatever the government wants done to the accused. I suspect that the government is unable to accomplish this goal in most of its sham trials.

As you can see, the selection process is clear-cut. It is not mysterious. But unless you know what is occurring, the process itself may act as a form of brainwashing. It is intended to have this effect on you so that you will be easier to control, so that your mind will be molded to be like that of the prosecutor, government attorney or attorney for the corporate giant.

"Your Honor, please don't let the jury know about our star witness' drug convictions; they won't believe him and we'll lose the case!"

Most ethical, conscientious citizens want to think that the entire process is honest and aboveboard. But you must attempt to be objective and to not involve yourself in the personalities of the judge or the attorneys. You should attempt to remain aloof so that you will not become biased or prejudiced to the point that you cannot make a just decision in the case.

You are not part of the judicial process in the sense of feeling welcome in the courthouse, although you help pay for the building and the salaries of the employees who work there. You are a "layman," a person who has not gone to law school. You are therefore regarded with contempt by the members of the bar who are present. Don't think for one second that everyone likes you and if you render a decision in favor of the government you will be regarded as "one of the boys." Regardless of what you do to ingratiate yourself with the court personnel, they will still wish they had never seen you and hope never to see you again. Of course, if you are going to make your decisions based upon whether the court personnel will be friendly with you in the future, you should not be a juror anyway.

# First
# Impressions

You have probably never been in a courtroom. As a result, you will be impressed by its formality. You have been taught (some would say programmed) to feel awe and unquestioning respect for everything that happens in court. Remember, judges are human beings, too. They sometimes commit crimes, but the news media do not usually give such failings adequate coverage. What this means is that you are deprived of access to information concerning the type of people with whom you are dealing.

Being selected as a juror involves you in a potentially dangerous situation. The honesty and ethics of judges and lawyers may sometimes leave something to be desired.

In many legal circles, jurors selected to hear a case are laughingly referred to as "twelve persons of equal ignorance." This is a fair comment if the jurors do not understand their rights and duties.

"The jury is the protection of your community against the prosecutor who sometimes abuses his power."[57] Occasionally federal or state attorneys fabricate a crime to obtain a conviction of someone speaking against their tyrannical practices. This is the "political crime." You should always watch for such abuses. The protection that you give to the community is derived from your common sense and the guarantee of the participation of members of your community in deciding who is really innocent or guilty.

In the case of Duncan v. Louisiana (1968) the judge stated:

> "The institution of trial by jury — especially in criminal cases — has its hold upon public favor chiefly for two reasons. The individual can forfeit his liberty — to say nothing of his life — only at the hands of those who, unlike any official, are in no wise accountable, directly or indirectly, for what they do, and who at once separate and melt anonymously in the community from which they came. Moreover, since if they acquit, their verdict is final, no one is likely to suffer of whose conduct they do not morally disapprove; and this introduces a slack into the enforcement of law, tempering its rigor by the mollifying influence of current ethical conventions."[58]

If the jury does not like the way the law is being enforced against a person accused of an offense, the jury can find that person not guilty. The "Not Guilty" verdict protects the accused from the oppressive acts of the government, represented at the trial by the prosecutor.

In an early case regarding the rights of juries, the court ruled that the jury's function was to accept the law given to it by the court and apply that law to the facts. The reason given was that the American Revolution was over and the people could trust their institutions. Nevertheless, the judge conceded that the jury had the right to disregard the judge's instructions and make its own decision.[59]

In the late 1800s the U.S. Supreme Court ruled that the jury was not to be given instructions that articulated a right to do whatever it willed.[60] That appears to be the rule today. The result is that a juror will not be told what his rights are by the judge or the attorneys. Therefore, **a juror must know what his rights are before he enters the courtroom.**

In 1969 a judge further explained this concept of keeping the juror's rights secret. He intimated that to tell the juror he can base his decision on whatever his conscience and common sense told him would invite anarchy.[61]

In other words, the juror, a wage earner just like you, is an ignorant anarchist only smart enough to pay the judge's salary through taxes, but is not smart enough to make an independent or fair decision.

"There they are, the jury panel,
*twelve people of equal ignorance!*"

In a trial, you are going to hear the facts of the case from the testimony of witnesses. The judge will explain the law in the case. You will have to put the law and the facts together to reach a verdict.

But **the jury is in no sense the agent of the judge**. Both the judge and the jury derive their origin from the same high source. In laying down rules to guide the jury in their deliberations, the judge merely acts as the mouthpiece of the law for the purpose of marking out a definite and clearly ascertained path by which the ends of justice are attained.[62]

Although the jury has the undisputed power to acquit even if its verdict is contrary to law as given by the judge and contrary to the evidence, the court will not tell the jurors their rights.[63] The judge will not tell the jurors that they may disregard the law and decide according to their preconceived opinions based upon personal experience or according to their consciences. They must learn about their rights and powers before they become jurors.

You the juror have powers but no information regarding what your powers are. For all practical purposes, these powers are hidden from you. Were you to participate in a trial as a juror without having the information concerning your duties, you might really harm someone relying upon you to be a fair and impartial juror. The crime of harming someone through ignorance is not armed robbery, but it is just as serious. When the judge makes comments that you don't like, or when he refuses to let you in on what you are supposed to do as a juror, the judge is manipulating you like a puppet.

If the jury is not told of its rights, but by some means learns about them and can utilize them, the law allows the jury to render any verdict, even if the verdict is illogical and inconsistent.[64] The protection of the community from harassment by government officials is assured if the potential jurors learn about their rights prior to being called to participate in a trial.

The jury has "an unreviewable and unreversible power . . . to acquit in disregard of the instructions on the law given by the trial judge . . . ."[65]

# Here's
# What To Do

It cannot be stressed too often that as a juror you must be fair and impartial. During the proceedings of the trial, you have two persons, the defense attorney and the prosecuting attorney, who will be making presentations. The defense attorney will be explaining to you why the accused is innocent. The prosecutor will be explaining why the accused is guilty.

The prosecutor and the judge are paid by the government. The defense attorney is probably being paid by the accused. If you consider this for a moment in the context of who has the most money to proceed as a party in the trial, the only answer available is that the prosecutor has the most money to obtain the conviction of the accused. He has not only the most money, but also has the staff and the resources of the government behind him. The accused has none of these things.

Trials in which the government is a party are always one-sided affairs. If the accused is a working man or woman, you can immediately understand the problem. If you had to hire an attorney at a rate of $200 to $300 per hour, could you afford the expense? That is why many people just plead "Guilty." The expense of a trial is worse than the punishment in many cases.

The generally accepted concept of two attorneys presenting their cases all by themselves appears to be fair. However, there cannot be fair trials in which the government is involved as long as this one-sided economic advantage exists. Further, the workload of the government attorney consists of cases on which the attorney still gets his salary, even if there is no activity for long periods of time. The private attorney representing a client is not in the same situation. Take this into account as you are making your decision in the case.

You should also consider what happened during the voir dire of the jury. Did the judge interfere with the questions asked by the defense attorney? Did the defense attorney ask each juror questions, or did he do a sloppy job by asking questions of the entire group of jurors?

You are going to have to evaluate whether the defense attorney has done a good job representing his client. If a person is represented by an attorney who does not do a good job, he is not adequately represented. If someone is inadequately represented in a trial, the question arises as to whether he has even had a trial. The trial itself is not a ritual of worship but is supposed to be an in-depth examination of the facts. If you are left with questions as to what has happened in a trial, then you have no basis upon which to make a decision of "Guilty."

When the judge and prosecutor are working together to obtain a conviction, the judge becomes an active participant in the trial. Under these conditions, the proceedings become little more than a farce. You the juror are being intimidated by such activities and you should find the accused "Not Guilty."

Our government is divided into three parts: the executive, the legislative and the judicial. Although each is a part of the government, they are supposed to operate independently as a system of checks and balances upon each other. Law enforcement is carried out by the executive branch. Writing of laws is carried out by the legislative branch. Administration of the system that determines

"Your Honor, you can tell by my client's face that he's innocent!"

whether a defendant has violated a law is the job of the judicial branch.

The judicial branch does not enforce the laws, and this is not the duty of the judge. If this occurs in the form of the judge explaining that his job is to enforce the laws, then you should find the accused "Not Guilty." The judge is using the court as a police apparatus like the "court" systems in the Soviet Union and other totalitarian regimes. Our American system of law prohibits such conduct.

If during the trial the judge tells you more than once to "disregard what you have just heard," then you can rest assured that some kind of conspiracy exists between the prosecutor and the judge. They are hiding evidence from you, probably very dramatic evidence, that would assist you in making a fair and just decision. As we all know, the best way to have someone remember something is by reinforcing it in their minds by telling them to disregard it.

It is easy for any of us to want to demonstrate that we understand concepts we really don't. In casual relationships with acquaintances, this practice really doesn't do any harm. However, as a juror you must understand the facts presented in the case. If you don't understand the facts, then you should find the accused "Not Guilty." It would be grossly dishonest to find someone "Guilty" if you did not understand the case.

When a jury is divided and cannot agree on a "Guilty" or "Not Guilty" verdict, the result is a "Hung Jury." It is regarded as the third verdict a jury can issue. The importance of a Hung Jury cannot be over-emphasized. Of course an additional trial may result, but it only means that adequate evidence and facts were not offered to the jury in the first place. A hung jury is the only logical result in such a case.

If your jury cannot reach a firm decision on guilt or innocence, the judge may attempt to force you into reaching a verdict you do not want to make. You should resist the temptation at all costs. If the jury is in this situation, other people on the jury will attempt to pressure you into voting with them. The pressure will build because you will be told that you can't go home until you make a decision. At this point, the trial ceases being a trial because your independence as a juror is being restricted. Under our system of law this is very bad.

You are a juror. You are not selling hamburger in the grocery store, nor are you negotiating the price of a sombrero in a Mexican market place. You are deciding if someone is going to be deprived of liberty and/or property. You need to emphathize with the accused. If you were the accused, would you want someone on the jury panel to try to give one of the jurors a sales job just so that juror could get home earlier for his ration of beer?

You must stick by your decision. You can tell the other jurors that you don't have to justify your decision to anyone. If they continue harassing and abusing you, say that you will tell the judge you have made a decision and the other jurors are trying to intimidate you into changing your mind. If things really start getting out of hand, never forget that the judge is not supposed to be imprisoning the jury.

You have made your decision; hopefully, it is based on a good understanding of what you have heard during the trial. If the judge and the other jurors persist in saying that everyone will have to stay until a decision is made, tell the judge that you wish to file a Writ of Habeas Corpus. Say that you are being illegally restrained and deprived of your

"I object! The jury should not be permitted to hear this evidence!"

liberty because you are being held prisoner by the judge. Write the statement on a sheet of paper in letter form and give it to the judge. Tell him that you wish to contact an attorney. You should also inform the defense attorney and the prosecuting attorney of the matter.

Under no circumstance should you just sit there and accept berating treatment from jurors who are more interested in going home to watch television than they are in performing their duties in an honorable and ethical manner.

In some trials, the jurors are given a list of questions to answer in the determination of guilt or innocence. This amounts to having the jury justify its decision, which it does not have to do. There is also a very serious language problem involved in a trial. The lawyers speak a special language. They probably understand the legal implications of what they are saying. The jury does not speak this specialized type of English. Consequently, when the written questions are given to the jury, the questions are not written in the same type of English that you have used throughout your life.

A communication problem exists that is very difficult to overcome. You are going to have to answer questions written in this legal language. Your own logic is different from the logic used to derive the questions. The judge may provide definitions of words and explanations of theories involved in this process, but he is explaining the matter to you in legal language and you are required to reach a decision using normal, everyday language and logic.

How can any valid decision be made under these circumstances? If this occurs and you do not understand, and no satisfactory explanation is given to you, then your vote should be "Not Guilty." Why should you permit your own lack of a legal education to be used in a way so that you become a pawn in such a fraud?

The key to this entire process is based upon what you, the juror, are willing to do. If you do not understand the case, it is not your fault. It is the fault of the attorneys involved. You must not penalize the accused if you do not understand the facts of the case, or if you feel there are large gaps in the information that has been presented to you.

Our system of law does not require a jury of lawyers. Consider for a moment why you did not attend law school. Perhaps you didn't want to study law. Perhaps your parents were not wealthy enough to send you to college. But you should never permit your lack of knowledge in technical legal theory to allow lawyers to use it to deceive you into making a decision based upon ignorance. There is nothing illegal about stating, "I don't understand." And there is nothing illegal about making the same statement after an "explanation" has been given to you ten times.

There are things that any normal person may never understand, especially when it is explained in a coded language such as legal language. The attorneys must provide you with an explanation that is sufficient for you to make a valid decision. Otherwise, you should find the accused innocent, or refuse to go along with the decision of the other jurors if they have decided to find him guilty.

Many jurors are jurors in name only because they allow themselves to be manipulated instead of demanding a satisfactory explanation of guilt or innocence.

If you feel there is something suspicious about the way the judge or the prosecutor is handling the case, find the accused "Not Guilty."

An integral part of the jury process is the effect of a "Guilty" or "Not Guilty" verdict. Most courts will refuse to give you this information. If this happens you should find the accused "Not Guilty." Many, many people have made decisions as jurors only to find that the result they intended was never accomplished. Under such circumstances, the juror should refuse to convict anyone because the juror has insufficient data upon which to send someone to jail.

Know what you are doing. Because many jury foremen are authority figures, i.e., such as executives of multinational corporations, banks, conglomerates or other enormous organizations, there is a tendency for the normal working man or woman to want to be accepted by that authority figure as an equal. This is manifested by a practice of agreeing with whatever the jury foreman states. Courts throughout history have always developed into the position of enforcing the will of the giant economic interests. One must be extremely careful not to become the puppet of such interests when one is a juror.

If the jury foreman is an employee of one of those

The guilty flee when Justice pursues them.

economic giants and the case involves an economic interest of that company, such as war or taxes, then the juror should be careful when the foreman tries to sell them his point of view.

In our society, war is beneficial to the large companies that obtain contracts from the government. High taxes fund the contract which the government hands out to its favorite corporate interests. In too many instances the government and the big corporations are on the same side.

The same thing applies to government employees who appear on juries. There is no way they can be fair-minded in questions involving the government. You, on the other hand, have to work for your salary. It has always been

The search continues for an unbiased, impartial juror.

questionable whether the activity in which government employees are involved, for which they receive a monthly check, is work or not.

A person receiving social security, for example, would not be very fair with someone who didn't like the Social Security system.

The attorney who launches a personal attack upon the honesty and integrity of a party to the suit, either prosecution or defense, probably has no case. In order to cover up a lack of evidence, he may use violent personal attacks. Name calling and terrible insults are common techniques. The juror may be tricked into overlooking the lack of evidence, and base his decision upon the drama of the personal attack. Jurors should beware of this technique. If it is used, the jury should merely find the party being

"Do you think the jury will understand questions written in Doublespeak?"

attacked "Not Guilty." The trial is not a personality contest, and it is dishonest to turn it into one.

When a final judgment is obtained in another state's jurisdiction, and is taken to your state to be enforced, it must first be given "full faith and credit" through a court proceeding. If you are a juror in such a matter, you should use extreme caution in making a decision. If the evidence upon which the judgment was based is not presented to you, you should not vote to give the out-of-state judgment full faith and credit. If the party who has the judgment in hand cannot prove to you that he deserves it, you should refuse to give it full faith and credit. After all, just because they were able to get a judgment against someone in another state does not mean that such a judgment would be acceptable to you in your state. Sometimes, the judge will merely order you to accept an out-of-state judgment. As stated before, you may ignore such instructions and arrive at your own independent decision.

As a juror, your responsibility is great. It is so great that if you participate in making a fraud of it, you are contributing to the destruction of our entire system of government. If the people do not have an organized forum in which to resolve their disputes, they might as well go into the streets and commit violence and destruction to achieve retribution for wrongs committed against them. That is why the American Revolution took place.

Your decision therefore should be an independent one, determined in accordance with your conscientiously held beliefs. This does not mean that you should ignore the instructions of the judge. You should consider them as you consider the facts of the case, and only then reach a decision you feel is fair and just. *You will want to make a decision that you can live with the rest of your life, without regret or excuse.*

# Summary

In this book we have examined the jury system from one specific vantage point: the concept of jury service as a fundamental right and responsibility of the citizens of a democratic society to ensure the liberty of its members. Human rights and our legal system have evolved together. An overview of their interworkings gives additional insight into the importance of the role of the juror.

The jury system developed as a substitute for the practice of families avenging injuries caused by one person against another. The substitution of a system where twelve persons determine guilt or innocence for a system of violence and vengeance killings is a milestone in the development of western society. Although its origins are uncertain, the mention of trial by jury in the Magna Carta in 1215 stresses its importance in the development of the concept of fundamental rights of man.

For such a system to function correctly, the community must have confidence in the system. The jury did not develop satisfactorily in England. It was strenuously controlled by the government. As stated at the beginning of this book, "trial by jury in England was merely a procedural farce utilized to resolve the disputes of the elite, and to legitimize the government oppression against the people by an 'official' act of a 'court.'"

One reason trial by jury became so ingrained in American jurisprudence is that it has actually been practiced here in a pure form. Although the jury process has occasionally fallen back into its historical use as an elitist institution, trial by jury remains one of the principal protections of our American system.

It is the duty of members of a free society to ensure that the jury is not utilized as a means to *legitimize* government oppression against the people, or as a way by which only the elite are able to resolve disputes.

To be a good juror, you must have a detailed knowledge of right and wrong. Traditionally, such information is found in the Bible. In addition, the first ten amendments to the U.S. Constitution are often called the fundamental freedoms of man. They provide a clear explanation of the individual's rights which should not be violated by the government. Since governments tend to develop into systems where the rights of the people are diminished, our Constitution was written with built-in provisions to prevent the government from getting out of control.

Internationally the concept of rights for the people of the Earth was set out in the Universal Declaration of Human Rights. This declaration defines in detail the rights of man.

After reading excerpts from the Bible, the Bill of Rights and the Universal Declaration of Human Rights, you should have a more complete understanding of right and wrong.

Many people have a general idea about these concepts, but before you become a juror, you should obtain a more specific understanding of them. By doing so you will be in a better position to participate in the decision-making process regarding the guilt or innocence of the accused. In other words, you need to take more with you to the jury than your body. You must take with you a base of knowledge concerning the matter in which you are involved.

Jurors are not supposed to be mere rubber stamps, approving whatever the government wants. Since you are the representative of the community, your job is to apply community standards in determining innocence or guilt. This also includes determining the fairness of the particular law under which the accused is being tried. If the juror feels that the law cannot be fairly applied to the accused, then the juror should find the accused innocent, even if he did, in fact, violate the law.

History includes many dramatic moments in which the accused were found innocent. These incidents swept the entire concept of the jury toward its ideal. Many jurors have had to stand against judges attempting to bully them into decisions the judges wanted.

The judge may try to persuade you and to advise you, but he cannot command you to make the decision he wants. He cannot coerce you or intimidate you into reaching the decision he desires.

Your decision is supposed to be fair and just and must be the product of your own independent judgment. There have been many laws that were bad. Historically, juries have disregarded bad laws. This is a valid function of the jury. Judges and the legal establishment dislike this because, as in all struggles for power, they prefer to be the ones in power - the elite. There is always the fear that having the people in control of the power centers will lead to anarchy, but our founding fathers felt that the people should have the final say as to what should be accepted as law. This means that the people, through the jury, even have the final decision on laws passed by Congress and the state legislatures. This power is in your hands when you become a juror.

Understand that not all judges and attorneys are unethical. The logical probability is that most of them are ethical and very dedicated to their work. For you to behave like any of the tyrants mentioned in this book makes you much worse than them, because the final ruling body on laws of this country is the jury.

When the Japanese were accused of violating the law requiring them to report to concentration camps, it was a jury that found them guilty. Can you imagine concentration camps in the United States? Jurors just like you found people guilty of violating such a horrible law. Would you think that a law which provided for sending members of religious groups to concentration camps is valid? If such a law did exist, your job would be to find the accused innocent. Our laws should not violate our basic concepts of freedom.

In all sincerity, if you believe in violating the rights of other people in this way, I suggest that you would be much happier if you sold all of your possessions and moved to the Soviet Union. You have no reason to be part of a jury if you do not believe in the fundamental freedoms of man which comprise the entire basis of our society.

In order to be a good juror, you must be a person of such high character that you will not permit the court to intimidate you. Your common sense is probably your best guide. I am constantly impressed by the deep understanding of life and society that people over the age of 50 possess. They are certainly an asset in the formulation of judgment regarding guilt or innocence.

A problematical situation arises in juries when the juror is either too eager to give in to opinions of stronger personalities, or is afraid to assert his own opinion. The result is the perversion of the jury process. The juror who feels that any decision is acceptable because he wants to hurry up and go home does a tremendous disservice to his community.

The fact that an unfair person participates in a generally fair procedure, such as trial by jury, is insufficient. That individual must be fair for the system itself to be fair. He who benefits from the openness of our society, but who is fearful of defending the rights that the people have accumulated over the centuries, is nothing more than a tyrant himself.

If a potential juror fears that if he makes a decision against the government then he will suffer harassment or punishment at the hands of government agents, that juror should tell the judge and the defense attorney that he is unable to objectively sit and make a decision in the case because of his fear of the government.

The selection of a jury is fairly simple. Lists are compiled by the particular authority responsible for selection of juries. These lists may be from voter registration lists or other lists that contain large numbers of names of residents of the areas concerned.

A notification is sent to prospective jurors, who then appear at the appointed place to go through the selection process. As a rule, if each juror is not asked questions individually by the attorney for the accused, then the accused has inadequate representation, and the entire trial may not be fair.

In federal court, the attorneys give lists of questions to the judge, who then reads the questions he feels are important to the jurors. This procedure is bad because the judge from the outset is becoming a participant in the trial instead of an impartial judge. Consequently, you should always be very suspicious about what is really going on during a federal trial. This is compounded by the peculiar selection process for federal juries. It attempts to fit potential jurors to a profile that is favorable to police statist attitudes, which applies to a person who is an employee of the government or who is employed by a multinational corporation. The government feels that these people are more inclined to agree with the position the government wants to take in a case. Hence, under those conditions, you should be very careful because the government is going to try to manipulate you like a puppet.

The courtroom may tend to make you feel disoriented because most people do not frequent the courts. The reason you will be treated with such great respect is not because the court personnel want to be friends with you. They treat you in this manner because of the honored position of jurors in our country. This misinterpretation of the procedures sometimes influences jurors in the sense that they want to repay the court personnel for treating them so nicely.

On the other hand, your position is a potentially dangerous one and can turn into a very nasty experience. So, you must not permit this first impression to influence your decision making.

You are the protection of the community against the arbitrary acts of government that, at times, turn our honorable procedures into acts of tyranny. That is why jurors can totally disregard what the judge tells them and find the accused innocent. Such a jury sends a definite message to the court, the government and law enforcement agencies to put a halt to their harassment of the community. You are not an agent of the judge, just as the judge is not an agent of the law enforcement community.

This rule is so strong that the jury can issue any verdict it desires, even if that verdict is illogical and inconsistent with the law.

Your initial impressions should not be permitted to put you into a state of mind that would interfere with the objectivity with which you view the facts of the case.

Practical considerations as to how a juror should conduct himself are usually never discussed. Being a juror is a serious activity and should be approached with that in mind. If the court impedes the trial by participating in it on the side of either of the parties, then there is an attempt to influence the juror to go support the attitude of the judge.

Adequacy of representation is important because if you feel that the accused is inadequately represented, then for all practical purposes there has not even been a trial. The jurors, in that situation, would not be able to find the accused guilty because he was inadequately represented.

The economic advantage of the government prevents trials from being fairly heard by a jury. This advantage interferes with the concept of jury trial.

The verdicts that a jury can issue are **Guilty**, **Not Guilty** and **Hung Jury**. The most interesting verdict is the last, because it signifies that sufficient information upon which to base a firm verdict was **not** provided to the jury.

Judges err when they try to force jurors to change their minds. This is done by intimidation, sales talks and telling the jury that deliberations must continue until a decision is reached, meaning that the jury may not be able to go home for days. Naturally, if you change your mind under these conditions, you are betraying our system of justice.

This book has informed you of the magnitude of the rights and powers of the jury so that if you are selected as a juror, you will be able to correctly perform your duties.

# Publisher's Afterword

Those who have worked on the production of this book feel that it addresses important social and political concerns. As a result, an unusual spirit of cooperation has existed during its editing and manufacture.

Our consensus is:

Given that a citizen supporting, and receiving the advantages of, a democratic social structure also assumes responsibility for its functioning; given that the jury system is a fundamental human right and the strongest check on governmental abuse; given that the jury system can function only in a society which fully supports it and makes available a pool of fair, competent and unbiased individuals to judge rightness and wrongness; then clearly our most basic responsibility, greatest opportunity and most important individual human right is to be a juror sitting in judgment on the law of the land.

Every year hundreds of thousands of people sit on juries in this country. Each should know the information contained in this book; few of them do. We ask that you pass this book along to a prospective juror. The survival of our mutual human rights may depend on it.

G. Nichols                                    March 1985

# Footnotes

1.  William Forsythe, M.A., <u>History of Trial by Jury</u> (New York: Burt Franklin, 1878), p. 46.
2.  Forsythe, p. 48.
3.  Ibid., p. 48.
4.  Ibid., p. 62.
5.  Ibid., p. 64.
6.  Ibid., p. 67.
7.  Louis B. Wright, <u>Magna Carta and the Tradition of Liberty</u> (Washington, D.C.: American Revolution Bicentennial Administration, 1976), p. 23.
8.  Hannis Taylor, <u>Origin and Growth of the English Constitution</u> (Boston: Houghton Mifflin Co., 1900), p. 374.
9.  Ibid., p. 374.
10. Thorne, Dunham, Kurland and Jennings, <u>The Great Charter</u> (New York: Pantheon Publications, 1965), p. 58.
11. <u>Bank of Columbia v. Okley</u>, 4 Wheaton 235, 244 (1819).
12. <u>Kennedy v. Mendoza-Martinez</u>, 372 US 144, 186 (1963).
13. Forsythe, p. 151.
14. <u>Declaration of Independence</u>, 1776.
15. <u>Van Ness v. Pacard</u>, 2 Peters 144 (1829).
16. <u>Massachusetts Colony Records</u>, V., (Boston: White Publishing, 1954), pps. 198, 200, 321.
17. Association of American Law Schools, <u>Select Essays in Anglo-American Legal History</u>, (Boston: Little, Brown and Co., 1907), p. 198.
18. Ibid., p. 198.
19. Ibid., p. 198.
20. Ibid., p. 198.
21. Ibid., p. 198.

22. Constitution of the United States of America.
23. The Holy Bible
24. The Holy Bible
25. The Holy Bible
26. The Holy Bible
27. The Holy Bible
28. The Holy Bible
29. Constitution of the United States of America, Amendments I through X
30. Universal Declaration of Human Rights, (New York: United Nations Office of Public Information, 1978).
31. US v. Moylan, 417 F.2d 1002 (CCA 4th, 1969).
32. James Alexander, A Brief Narrative of the Case and Trial of John Peter Zenger (Boston: Harvard University Press, 1963), p. 93.
33. Bushell's Case, 6 Howell's State Trials 999 (1670).
34. Ibid., p. 999.
35. Ibid., p. 999.
36. Josiah Quincy Reports, 21 Howell's State Trials 847 (1783).
37. Dean of St Asaph's Case, 21 Howell's State Trials 847 (1783).
38. State of Georgia v. Brailsford, et al, 3 US 1 (1794).
39. Horning v. District of Columbia, 254 US 135 (1920).
40. Moylan, p. 1002.
41. Horning, p. 135.
42. Fugitive Slave Act of 1850, 9 US Statutes at Large 462.
43. Rev. Charles Beecher, The Duty of Disobedience to Wicked Laws (New York: J.A. Gray, Printer, 1851).
44. US et rel. McCann v. Adams, Warden, et al, 126 F.2d 774 (CCA 2nd, 1942).
45. US v. Fielding, 148 FS 46 (USDC-DC, 1957).
46. Duncan v. Louisiana, 391 US 145 (1968).

47. Ibid., p. 155.
48. US v. Spock, 416 F.2d 165 (CCA 1st, 1969).
49. Ibid., p. 165.
50. Jessica Mitford, The Trial of Dr. Spock (New York: Alfred A. Knopf, 1969), p. 224.
51. US v. Davis, 413 F.2d 148 (CCA 4th, 1969).
52. US v. Garaway, 425 F.2d 185 (CCA 9th, 1970).
53. US v. Sawyers, et al, 423 F.2d 1335 (CCA 4th, 1970).
54. Huffman and Huffman v. US, 297 F.2d 754 (CCA 5th, 1962).
55. Korematsu v. US, 323 US 214 (1944).
56. G.T. Munsterman, C.H. Mount and William R. Pabst, Jr., Multiple Lists for Juror Selection: A Case Study for San Diego Superior Court (Washington, D.C.: LEAA, 1978), p. C-1.
57. Duncan, p. 145.
58. McCann, p. 774.
59. US v. Battiste, 2 Sum. 240, Fed. Cas. No. 14,545 (CCD Mass., 1835).
60. Sparf v. US, 156 US 51 (1895).
61. Moylan, p. 1002.
62. Henry Edward Randall, Instructions to Juries(Kansas City, Missouri: Vernons Law Book Co., 1922).
63. Moylan, p. 1002.
64. Horning, p. 138.
65. US v. Dougherty, 473 F2d 1132 (CCA DC, 1972).

# Index